Writing Rules!

The grammar, spelling,
punctuation,
and encouragement
you need to
do well on
standardized tests,
write good essays,
and lead a
long and healthy life.

Charles Gulotta

Writing Rules!
Copyright © 2010 by Charles Gulotta.
All rights reserved.
Published by Mostly Bright Ideas.
Printed in the United States of America.

No portion of this book may be reproduced in any form without written permission of the author.

This is the first edition.

ISBN-10: 0-9653263-7-3
ISBN-13: 978-0-96532-637-7

All of the illustrations in this book came from iclipart.com.

It's time to learn this stuff once and for all. You haven't learned it yet because it hasn't been important enough. Since the first time you heard these rules in school, you've listened to thousands of songs, watched hundreds of television shows and movies, decided what to wear and where to eat, figured out how to download music, changed your ringtone, sent your friends nine million meaningless text messages, and made countless decisions about countless things you can't even remember now. And still you confuse *their* and *there*. Let's fix it.

Contents

Introduction 5

The Rules
Apostrophes, Contractions, and Other Headaches 10
Spelling, and Why It Matters 12
What About the Rules? 13
Double Consonants 14
Where Does It End? (Part 1) 15
Where Does It End? (Part 2) 16
What's the Word? 18
Dumber & Dumbest 27
As & Like 27
Redundancy 28
One Word or Two? 30
What Are You Talking About? 34
Fragments, Run-ons, & Compound Sentences 35
It's Right Because It's Right (Usage) 38
Just Between You and Me 39
A Lesson from the Mailbox 41
Can We Reach an Agreement? 43

Verb Tenses 46
Infinitive or *-ing* Verb? 49
Grammar is a Parallel Universe 50
Putting Modifiers in Their Place 52
Don't Change Your Voice 53
Neither-Nor, Either-Or 53
The Elusive Semicolon 54
Ifs, Ands, & Buts 55
Hopefully, An Answer to the Adverb Question 56
The Mysterious *They* 58
Possessive + Gerund 59

Practice Questions
Part 1: Finding the Error 60
Part 2: Fixing the Error 71
Part 3: Paragraphs 81

Essays 94
Essay 1 97
General Rules for the Essay 102
Essay 2 104
Before & After 109

Rules We Don't Need 110
A Few More Suggestions and Reminders 112
And a Few More Challenges 114
What is Writing Made Of? 118

Introduction

Have you ever gone to the dentist and had a fluoride treatment? Wasn't it hideous? Doesn't the thought of it make you want to get up right now and run around the room flapping your arms?

What does that have to do with writing? Nothing. But I know that reading this book is a burden and you're dreading it. Grammar, spelling, and punctuation. Sentence structure. Verb tenses. You've heard this stuff a million times. It's dry and lifeless. It's the last thing you want to be doing. What could possibly be worse? I think we both know the answer to that: fluoride.

Let's review. So far we've established that learning about writing is preferable to swishing a disgusting thick liquid around in your mouth. But at least that unpleasant task has some purpose; if we can believe the dentist, it helps keep our teeth from rotting away and falling out of our mouths. What is this writing thing anyway?

Writing is a tool that allows one mind to communicate with another, without talking. Why do we need tools? First, because we can't read each others' minds. Second, our minds are not coherent; they're random and scattered. We think in abbreviated and overlapping images, sounds, concepts, and memories. Thoughts appear in bursts, like fireworks, frequently unannounced ("Hey, great picnic last Tuesday!" "My ear hurts." "Stupid car." "I wonder where the cat's been for the past three days." "Spaghetti tonight?") These thoughts leave impressions that we can store and later retrieve from memory, sometimes. But they're almost never represented by clear words, phrases, and sentences. And again, we don't have total control of our thoughts. I seem to have very little control, but that's me. I don't know about you.

Which is exactly the point. We live in our own minds. It's a comfortable and familiar place. But what does it feel like to be in another person's head? What really goes on in there? We can never know for sure, and it's probably just as well. We're all pretty much trapped in our own mental landscape.

This isolation works fine as long as we want to keep our thoughts to ourselves. But when we need to convey some of our ideas to another person, we have to give them structure. Otherwise we'd sound like babbling idiots. If the person is standing right next to us, we try to translate the ideas into understandable speech. If the person is far away, or will be receiving our thoughts at a later time, we usually resort to this act called writing.

Our goal, then, is to take these random, incoherent, abstract thoughts and give them order and precision, putting them down in such a way that they can be decoded later by someone reading the words. The reader, then, comes to understand the thoughts of the writer. Two minds -- disconnected and perhaps strangers to each other -- connect, and become familiar. At least a little.

So what? Why is that so important? Well, say you're locked in a small room with a ticking explosive device and a set of instructions for disabling the bomb. And let's also say that the person who wrote the instructions is not so good with words. His grammar is shaky, and he writes *of* when he means *off*, and *to* when he means *two*. Wouldn't you start to get irritated with him after a short while? You'd find yourself wishing he'd paid more attention in English class, and at least made an attempt to proofread his work. You'd also find yourself sweating a lot. Clear and concise writing would suddenly seem like the most important thing in the world.

Most situations are not that urgent or life-threatening. Still, in the effort to get one mind to understand the thoughts of another, good writing is always better than bad. Communication isn't easy. You've had this experience before, when you were sure the other person got what you were saying, only to find out later that they had no idea what you were talking about. And they were standing right there. You were looking them in the eye and they were nodding in agreement. Surely your minds had connected. Then they walked away and behaved as if you'd said the exact opposite of what you did say. Like when you try to tell someone they have some food on their face. Don't they always reach for the wrong side? You move your hand up, they move theirs down. You've played telephone: a small circle of people relay a simple message, and by the time it goes around once it's completely distorted. Now imagine how much misunderstanding could occur between writer and reader, with only printed words to bridge the gap.

Writing allows us to tell stories, report news, and convey information. Without it, we'd have to rely on oral communication. And with the faulty listening skills and memory problems most people exhibit, that wouldn't work very well. So we need to write. But the world has enough gibberish. In other words, we need to write *well*. And for that, we need rules.

How many rules are there? Thousands. Rules about spelling, punctuation, grammar, and usage. Rules with names like Subjunctive Mood, Intransitive Verbs, and Future Perfect Tense. And of course, there are the countless exceptions to the rules. To add a final helping of confusion, the English language is constantly evolving. When has a rule officially changed? Is it all right to use slang? Which is more important, correctness or clarity?

And who decides what is and isn't good writing? There are rules you should never break, others you can break in certain situations, and still others that aren't really rules. This paragraph, for example, begins with the word *And*. I've had teachers who would have taken off points for that, and others who wouldn't have cared, or even noticed. Are you working on an essay for a college application? Taking the SAT? Writing a short story for a creative writing class? Or sending an email to your friend in Oklahoma? Just as the rules for speech are different from the rules for writing, there are different rules for writing, depending on who the reader will be.

Whether you're dealing with an unbreakable rule, a vague or debatable rule, or a rule that isn't a rule at all, it helps to be aware of them. Then, if you choose to violate or ignore one, you can do it with confidence, not to mention a little elegance.

In this book, we'll tear it down and put it back together in ways that, I hope, make more sense. We'll label and explain the most commonly-broken rules. We'll do practice questions and highlight ways to immediately see what you should be focused on. We'll emphasize the things you have to do in order to improve your writing and score higher on standardized tests. We'll identify those situations that permit a relaxed style, and those that require stricter formality. And we'll examine some writing samples in an effort to decide where the boundaries are: what is universally-accepted to be good writing and what isn't. We'll start simple, with the things you absolutely have to start doing right now. Then we'll move on to the rules and some more complicated stuff.

We're also going to work through a few essays. We'll begin with sample prompts, such as those you'd get on the SAT. Then we'll figure out how to approach the essay, write a draft, and correct those inevitable clumsy sentences and grammatical errors.

Why do we keep making the same mistakes over and over? I'll tell you. It's because we focus on what we want to avoid. A policeman once explained to me that people will often drive their car into a tree that stands alone in a field. Looking at the scene later, you think, "Wow, how did he hit that?" He hit it because when he lost control of the car, the first thing he looked at was the tree. Then he thought to himself, "Man, I really don't want to drive in that direction." And then he drove precisely in that direction; he slammed into the very thing he was trying to avoid.

I know this is starting to sound like self-help, positive thinking mumbo-jumbo. Believe me, I'm not into that. But it *is* true: We think about what we don't want to do, then we head straight for it.

Most books that try to help you stop making mistakes keep showing you the mistakes. So you're always looking at the very thing you want to stop doing. True, they also show you the correct way, but it's up to you to remember which is which. It's memorization, and we both know how well that works.

People who read a lot don't have this problem. They have seen correct spelling, vocabulary, grammar, punctuation, and usage so many times that they can spot a mistake right away and recognize it for what it is. If you saw a zebra with green stripes, you would question it immediately, because you've seen a real zebra often enough (at least in pictures).

So the long-range remedy for bad writing is to read more. Read a variety of things, and pay attention to how ideas are expressed. Are the sentences all long or short? Does the writer use punctuation well? Is the vocabulary appropriate for the topic, or is the author just showing off? Can you understand what you're reading the first time, or do you have to keep rereading?

Well, great. After five or six years you'll have a much better grasp of the language and how to use it yourself. But you need some help now, don't you? Isn't that why you're reading this, and not out playing rugby or watching some mind-expanding sitcom from the 1980s?

This book explains a bunch of things you can do immediately. You've heard some of them before. Many times. Make a conscious and sincere decision to learn them once and for all. It's much easier to learn something once (a zebra has black stripes) than to have to keep looking it up, endure being corrected, or unknowingly appear ignorant.

Each concept, rule, or suggestion has a box next to it. Like this:

☐ When you're sure you've learned the idea, put a check mark in the box. You won't need to waste time going over it again later. When you feel confident enough, move on to later sections to learn similar concepts about putting together sentences, paragraphs, and essays.

Pay attention to style, tone, and voice. Concentrate on identifying what you want to say and how you want to say it. And remember, this really is an endless pursuit. Writing is like racquetball -- you can learn the basics quickly, but you'll spend a lifetime making subtle improvements and mastering new skills. One of my college professors used to say, "Good plays aren't written. They're rewritten." That advice applies to any form of writing, including novels, short stories, poems, biographies, essays, magazine articles, letters to the editor, radio commercials, and soup can labels. It's a process, and very often -- maybe even most of the time, and with most writers -- that first draft isn't so hot. The second draft is a little better, and the third and fourth are better still.

This need for revision is one of the problems I have with the writing sections of standardized tests. The element of time is such a major factor on these tests that they don't necessarily allow the test-taker's writing skills to materialize. Unless you're dealing with a tight deadline, what does time have to do with writing? How long did it take Shakespeare to write *Hamlet*? No one knows, or cares. It's the finished product that matters. But on the SAT and other tests, there's no time or space for rewriting. The focus is on form: did you answer the question, did you deliver your message competently, and did you do so without breaking any major grammar laws?

All the more reason to learn the rules now, while you have time. Rules don't have to be intimidating. Actually, they're liberating. When you no longer have to waste energy thinking about the basics, you can focus on what you want to say. It's like cooking. If you can learn how many ounces are in a pint, you won't have to look it up anymore, and you can spend your time finding new recipes and adding your own flavors. (In some ways, it's better than cooking. When you write, you don't get raw egg stuck between your fingers.)

On the pages that follow you'll find examples of errors I see all the time, not only from students, but from adults, too (including some teachers, and other people who should know better). Make a decision to learn the rules once, and you'll avoid making these mistakes for the rest of your life. Why should you care? Because no matter how great your writing is otherwise, no matter how stunningly-creative your ideas, misspelling a word or using the wrong verb tense can send a signal to your reader that you may not really know what you're talking about. Your credibility will be blown. And who wants that?

Even though we'll be going through pages and pages of common mistakes, we'll try to stay focused on how to write correctly. With a little luck, we won't slam into too many trees. In the end, you still may not love writing, but you should be able to approach it with less fear and greater confidence.

Come on. It'll be more fun than fluoride, I can promise you that. Don't forget to rinse.

The Rules

Apostrophes, Contractions, and Other Headaches

Contractions and their obnoxious little friends (*it's* and *its*, for example) are confusing for a lot of people. I think it's because of the apostrophes. Apostrophes cause trouble. Somehow they make our brains rotate inside our skulls, and we end up doing everything backwards. That's why you see signs hanging in store windows that say, "Watermelon's $3 each!" and "Its always a good time to check your cars tire's!"

A **contraction** is a word that has been shortened by removing a letter or two. The apostrophe shows where those missing letters would have (or would've) been.

An apostrophe is also used to indicate the **possessive form of a noun**: George's hat, the giraffe's tail, Germany's southern border.

The possessive form of a pronoun does *not* get an apostrophe: hers, yours, ours. And you almost never need an apostrophe to change a noun from singular to plural.

Learn those few simple rules and you'll avoid making so many of the mistakes common in public communication these days. Here's a quick lesson on plurals, apostrophes, and contractions.

To change a singular noun to plural, you usually add *-s* or *-es*:
  "Would someone please get these *boxes* off my foot?"
  "My uncle was born in the *1800s*. His seven *sons* are all dead."
  "Are your *dogs* going to bark like that through the entire wedding?"

Use an apostrophe to form a contraction:
  "I *can't* believe *you're* wearing that shirt to your graduation."
  "*We've* been waiting here for twelve days."
  "Do you think *she's* going to notice that llama in the garage?"

And use an apostrophe to form a noun's possessive:
  "Are you going to *Francis's* retirement party?"
  "I think my *cat's* behavior is becoming a little peculiar."
  "Excuse me, sir, but this is the *children's* department."

Possessive pronouns are already possessive (no apostrophes needed):
  "Those forks are *ours*."
  "That knife is *theirs*."
  "This spoon is *yours*."
  "*Whose* corkscrew is that?"

Writing Rules!

☐ The word is *you're*. It's a contraction and it means *you are*.
"My, that's a pretty big burrito you're eating, Brian!"
"Frank, you're the hairiest person I've ever met."
"Thank you for coming, Felicia. You're just in time to help me shampoo the carpeting."

☐ The other word is *your*. It's used to indicate possession.
"I think your dog is up in that tree."
"May I borrow your orange sweater for the Halloween party?"
"I can tell by the look on your face that you don't like squid."

☐ The word *it's* is a contraction, and it means *it is*.
"It's another fine day for a car wash, isn't it, Claire?"
"I think it's time to clean out the refrigerator."
"It's a real shame what happened to your tricycle, Timmy."

☐ The other word is *its*. This word indicates possession.
"That goldfish has jumped out of its tank for the last time."
"The full moon seems to have cast its spell on the entire town."
"Mr. O'Brien's front door just blew off its hinges. Again."

☐ *They're* is a contraction, and means *they are*.
"They're members of a cult that eats only yellow food."
"I hope they know what they're doing with those hand grenades."
"Did you hear about the Boyles? They're moving to Montana."

☐ *Their* indicates possession.
"Why do they keep parking their truck on our porch?"
"They wore hip boots to the mall, but their English was perfect."
"They never returned our rake, so I stole their pool."

☐ *There* refers to location or existence.
"Jenny, go over there and tell those men you're sorry."
"There isn't nearly enough room in here for that cow."
"They're saying their parakeet flew into that field over there."

☐ *Who's* is a contraction for *who is*. *Whose* is a possessive pronoun.
"Who's going to be first to try my dandelion soup?"
"Whose pants are those on top of the microwave?"

Writing Rules!

Spelling, and Why It Matters

We live in a world in which email and texting (and probably something new that I don't know about) are important ways to communicate. The emphasis is often on information and speed, and spelling takes a backseat. Or gets thrown into the trunk.

That's fine if the context is a short message between friends. But when working on an essay or any other piece of writing that may have some effect on your future, make it as perfect as you can. Misspelled words are like dirty clothes: they create an impression, and not a good one. They tell the reader that you're sloppy, that you didn't give this piece of writing your best effort, and that maybe it isn't all that important to you.

Misspellings also damage your credibility. Say I'm a magazine editor and you send me an article you've written on some environmental issue. If you repeatedly spell *environment* incorrectly, what am I going to think about how careful you were with your research? Your facts may be triple-checked and right on the mark, but I'll have my doubts.

Here are a few common mistakes. No doubt the list could be much longer, and is probably endless, but we have to start somewhere. Let's start with these. Check the box when you're sure you've learned all five.

☐ **calendar.** This word is often misspelled with *-er* at the end, possibly because the last four months of the calendar all end with those letters. But you know how to spell *year*. Connect *calendar* with *year* and remember thay both end with *-ar*.

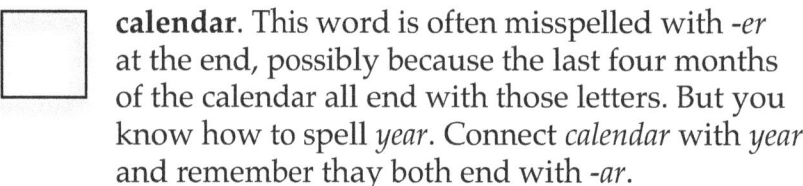

separate. I learned this trick from my sixth-grade English teacher. The word *separate* has two *e's* separated by two *a's*. Get it? (Notice I used an apostrophe to create a plural of individual letters -- one of the few times it's okay to do so. Writing *es* and *as* could be confusing.)

cemetery. Not sure why this is a tough one, but it is. People want to put an *a* at the end. Don't. If you think of a cemetery as a scary place, just imagine a scream ("eee!") and you'll get it right.

occasion. Just go by the pronunciation. If it had two *s's*, it would rhyme with *passion*. Which it doesn't. And speaking of *rhyme*, it rhymes with *thyme*.

forty. It's different from four, just as twenty is different from two and thirty is different from three. No *u* -- what's so hard?

Writing Rules!

What About the Rules?

Hey! We were promised rules! Where are they? Okay, here's the thing. The English language has rules for spelling, but everyone who knows them has been dead for at least eighty years.

I have to be honest: that's not completely true. There are a few rules we can talk about. But these rules all have exceptions. A lot of them. And the problem with a rule that has a lot of exceptions is that after a while, it doesn't seem like a rule anymore.

The spelling rule we all learned in school is "I before E, except after C." That sounded pretty good. Short, simple, and it rhymes, which makes it easier to remember. But then there was that second verse: "And when sounding like A, as in *neighbor* and *weigh*." It turned out there was a whole list of words that had a sound like A: sleigh, eight, freight, vein, rein, beige, feign, heinous, and quite a few others.

This "I before E, except after C" rule does help us correctly spell many common words. For example: relief, believe, niece, chief, field, yield, and hygiene. And when they follow C: receive, deceive, perceive, ceiling, receipt, and so on. The problem appears when we deal with the exceptions -- because there are so many of them, and because they're words we use all the time. Here are just a few of the words that have E before I, even though they don't follow C and they don't have the long A sound: foreign, seize, height, either, neither, leisure, forfeit, counterfeit, sleight, protein, caffeine, sovereign, veil, seismic, heir, and weird. And then there are the words that have I before E even though they follow C: proficient, efficient, sufficient, science, species, and on and on.

Where does this leave us? With lists of words to learn. Ultimately, it comes down to recognizing the correct spelling when you see it, and developing the ability to look at a word and just know when it isn't right. It has to do with memory. When you see a house that you've passed by a hundred times, you instantly know if it's been painted a different color. That's because the familiar image is stored in your brain. When you hear a favorite song performed by a different artist, it doesn't sound the same as the version you're used to, and something about it bothers you (that isn't how it's supposed to sound). You can do the same with spelling, but it requires that crucial step of first becoming familiar with the words. And that, I'm sorry to have to say one more time, involves reading. A great deal of reading.

The following pages talk about other kinds of words we frequently misspell. I've broken them down into a few categories, but there are always the strays that defy categorization. We'll end with a large list of troublesome words, including the ones we've already talked about on this page. Such a list can never be complete, but I think it's a good start. Spell these correctly and you will have made a decent dent in the problem. Stay with it.

Double Consonants

Almost everyone has trouble with these. Look on a few tourism websites and you'll quickly spot the word *accommodations* spelled with one M. Pick up a magazine on astronomy and you may see *satellite* misspelled. In fact, the word *misspelled* itself is on almost every list of problem words.

What is it about double consonants? I think it's that in some words, double consonants make a difference in how the word is pronounced, and often result in a completely different word. When you add a second P to *super*, it changes the long U sound to a short U, producing *supper*. But in many other words, double consonants don't seem to serve any purpose. In *necessary*, for example, why are the double S's necessary? Why does *millennium* need two L's?

Sometimes, it seems as though the wrong consonant has been doubled. If I had my way, the word *personnel* would have one N and two L's. And *parallel* would end with -lell. These are the real troublemakers. The words that, if spelled differently, would still be pronounced the same, and would pretty much still look right. *Sheriff*. Give it two R's and one F, and it sounds like the same word. But it would be wrong.

Occasionally, knowing how to spell one word can lead you to misspelling another. *Withhold*, for example, has those two H's in the middle, which is kind of unusual. The word *threshold*, on the other hand, doesn't. *Roommate* is troublesome (as many roommates are), and so is *bookkeeper*. A few more:

accidentally	**graffiti**	**questionnaire**
accommodate	**harass**	**recommend**
address	**immediate**	**referral**
aggressive	**intelligent**	**roommate**
beginning	**irregular**	**satellite**
bookkeeper	**Mediterranean**	**sheriff**
broccoli	**millennium**	**skillful (or skilful)**
Caribbean	**necessary**	**successful**
committee	**occurrence**	**suppress**
dumbbell	**opposition**	**tobacco**
embarrass	**parallel**	**tomorrow**
exaggerate	**personnel**	**tyranny**
giraffe	**possession**	**withhold**

There are plenty of rules concerning double consonants, and you'll have no trouble finding them elsewhere. But I think it's far easier (and less confusing) to acquaint yourself with the individual words -- learn their look.

Where Does It End?
Part 1
-able or -ible

Here we go again. There are hundreds of adjectives that end in either *-able* or *-ible*. These words describe the ability to do something, and usually have a verb as their root. For example, *curable* refers to the ability to be cured. *Accessible* describes the level to which something can be accessed.

So far, so good. Once again, however, the rules are the problem. The endings sound the same. So how do you decide which suffix to use?

It depends on which expert you ask. Some will tell you that if the root is a complete word by itself, use *-able*. If not, use *-ible*. That does work quite often (*passable, dependable*) and (*compatible, invincible*). But here come the exceptions. Why is it *applicable*? *Applic* is not a word. And what about *digestible*? *Digest* is a word, so shouldn't it end with *-able*?

Other experts say the rule is based on whether the root word comes from Latin or French. Assuming you're able to tell if a word comes from Latin or French (I can't, and I was an altar boy in the '60s), I still doubt you'll find much online clarity. Some websites tell you that *-able* words come from Latin, while others insist it's the *-ible* words that do. (As if we weren't confused enough already.) I don't think we need to go any further with that one.

There are still other rules concerning the last letter of the root. If the word ends in *-y*, do this, but if it ends in *-ss*, do that, and if it ends in *-e*, do something else. Don't forget the exceptions.

The one glimmer of hope I can offer is that most of these words end in *-able*. That means if you can learn to recognize the shorter list of *-ible* words, you can assume the others end in *-able,* and you'll be right most of the time. Also remember that new words (*clickable, biodegradable, networkable*) almost always end with *-able.*

Here's that list:

accessible	**divisible**	**incredible**	**plausible**
admissible	**edible**	**indefensible**	**possible**
audible	**eligible**	**indestructible**	**reprehensible**
collapsible	**feasible**	**infallible**	**responsible**
combustible	**flexible**	**invincible**	**reversible**
compatible	**gullible**	**invisible**	**sensible**
deductible	**horrible**	**irresistible**	**susceptible**
digestible	**illegible**	**negligible**	**tangible**
discernible	**imperceptible**	**permissible**	**terrible**

Where Does It End?
Part 2
-ance or -ence

As you've no doubt guessed by now, the rules for this one are useless, too. Again, they're based on Latin, and I don't even know what they are. Beware also of self-proclaimed linguistics experts who tell you there's a clear-cut rule (similar to the unreliable one regarding *-able* and *-ible*) that says if the root is a complete word, use *-ance*; if not, use *-ence*. Sure, this works with many words: *assistance, importance, resistance* and *independence, intelligence, violence*. But what about *nuisance, ambulance,* and *significance*? Their roots aren't complete words, so the ending should be *-ence*. And look at *preference, existence,* and *deference*; all have complete roots, so according to the rule should end in *-ance*. But they don't.

The real answer to these spelling issues is, by now, a familiar one. The more you read, the more frequently you'll see these words, and the more they'll be burned into your long-term memory. Here's a list of some of the more common examples. You could probably double this list on your own with a single day's reading.

abundance	guidance	absence	incoherence
acceptance	hindrance	adherence	independence
alliance	ignorance	adolescence	inference
ambulance	importance	affluence	influence
annoyance	inheritance	ambivalence	innocence
appearance	insurance	benevolence	intelligence
appliance	maintenance	circumference	interference
acquaintance	nuisance	competence	lenience
assistance	observance	conference	magnificence
assurance	performance	confidence	negligence
attendance	radiance	correspondence	obedience
balance	reluctance	credence	patience
clearance	relevance	deference	preference
defiance	resemblance	difference	prevalence
distance	resistance	diligence	prominence
dominance	significance	divergence	redolence
elegance	substance	eloquence	reference
endurance	tolerance	essence	sequence
fragrance	variance	existence	turbulence
grievance	vigilance	experience	violence

One More List

We do need to get back to the rules, but there are more spelling words we should at least acknowledge (hey, there's one now). These are words that are hard to put into a category. They're just troublesome for their own individual reasons. And for all I know, you may disagree. It's possible that you'll look over this list and think, what's he talking about? These are easy. I hope so. But somebody out there is having a problem with these words, because I see them misspelled all the time. Take a look and see what you think.

acknowledgment
acquire
acquaintance
apparent
Arctic
argument
barbecue
camouflage
column
congratulate
conscience
conscientious
consensus
copyright
definitely
despair
discipline
environment
exhilarating
extrovert
fiery
fluorescent
fulfill
gauge
government
grateful
hindrance
hypocrisy
introvert
judgment
knowledge

license
maneuver
mathematics
memento
minuscule
mischievous
mortgage
nauseous
noticeable
opportunity
pastime
perseverance
playwright
precede
prerogative
privilege
proceed
pursue
refrigerator
repetition
restaurant
rhythm
sacrifice
sacrilegious
sergeant
supersede
surprise
tariff
temperature
truly
vacuum

Mildly Interesting

In English, two words are often combined to form one. When the last letter of the first word is the same as the first letter of the second word, we sometimes keep both, giving us a double consonant:

bookkeeper
dumbbell
newsstand
roommate
withhold

But sometimes we drop one of the letters:

pastime
threshold

What's the Word?

A common writing mistake is to use the wrong word. You might think of this as a spelling error, and it may be. Or you may realize you're dealing with two different words, but just choose the wrong one. In any case, here are some traps to avoid. As always, there are more, but these are some of the most common. And spell-checkers won't help.

☐ The word *than* is used for comparisons.
"A school bus is larger than a pineapple."
"I would rather eat sawdust than another piece of this cake."
"It's hotter than a barbecue in that room."

☐ *Then* refers to a sequence in time.
"First you pay your rent, then I give back your blender."
"Put your socks on, then your shoes."
"What did you do then, Dad, after you got hit by the lightning?"

☐ *To* is a preposition. It's used to help indicate movement or direction.
"Marcia drove all the way to Indiana with her turn signal on."

☐ *Too* means also, or indicates an excessive degree.
"Dave ate too much cotton candy, and I think I did too."

☐ *Two* is a number and it comes right after one. You knew that.
"According to this ad, if you buy two dishwashers, you get one free."

The mistake here almost always involves using *to* when *too* would be correct. I don't think I've ever seen it the other way around.

☐ *Lose* is a verb, and it means to misplace, or to go from a condition of having to a condition of not having something.
"If you lose that briefcase, Bill, you'll also lose your job."

☐ *Loose* is an adjective. It means not tight.
"Mondays are pretty loose, and I take a four-hour lunch."

Again, the problem usually involves using *loose* when the word should be *lose*. No one ever writes, "This shirt is too lose."

☐ *Led* (pronounced LED) is the past tense of the verb *lead* (LEED).
"He led us out of the mall, and for that we will be forever grateful."
"Ira said he'd lead us to the spot where he buried the stolen toasters."

☐ *Lead* pronounced (LED) is a noun, and refers to a dense, gray metal.
"No offense, Pete, but these cupcakes taste like lead."

The error usually occurs when the writer uses *lead* instead of *led*. And the cause of the trouble, I think, is actually the verb *read*. The present tense of *read* (pronounced REED) is used like this: "I like to read when I'm eating alone." Here's the problem. The past tense of *read* is spelled the same, *read*, but pronounced RED: "I'm pretty sure I read that book in the second grade."

Another little quirk in the language. Confusing, but not a big deal.

☐ *Affect* (with the stress on the second syllable) is usually used as a verb:
"A steady diet of marshmallows will eventually affect your health."

But it can also be a noun, meaning a pretended behavior (stress on the first syllable):
"His phony affect, that of the miserable artist, got on our nerves."

☐ *Effect* is usually used as a noun:
"The boss's non-stop screaming had a negative effect on the staff."

But it can also be a verb, meaning to bring about:
"Marty was able to effect a happier marriage by selling his golf clubs."

☐ Use *between* when talking about two things or two people.
"If I had to pick between the two extremes, I'd rather be filthy rich."

Use *among* when discussing three or more.
"It was hard to choose the best meatloaf among the dozens of entries."

☐ *Take* something from here to there.
"Take this ironing board over to Mrs. Beedy and say happy birthday."

Bring something from there to here.
"I'd appreciate it, Earl, if you'd bring my piano back."

☐ *Principal* can be either a noun or adjective. As a noun, it refers to a main participant in some situation. For example, the two sides in a trial or boxing match would be the principals of those events. As an adjective, it means most important or influential.
"The principals in the debate all came across as boring and stupid."
"Our principal reason for being here was, frankly, the free food."

☐ A *principle* is a law, rule, or fundamental truth on which other beliefs are based. It is always a noun.
"He lacks moral principles, and that's why he set fire to your tent."

☐ When you have things that can be counted, use *fewer* or *number*. If it's a mass quantity, use *less* or *amount*.

"Why do I always get fewer cookies than Hank does?"
"I believe this elevator was built for a smaller number of people."
"Feel free to give me less squash if there isn't enough. Really, I insist."
"What's the correct amount of water for this much cement, Sid?"

☐ *Stationery* is a noun and refers to stuff you write on (letterhead, envelopes, cards). Connect it to the word *paper* -- both have -*er*.
"Ron, this new stationery has our logo upside-down."

☐ *Stationary* is an adjective; it means motionless. I have actually seen this word misused on boxes of printer paper. Maybe the boxes weren't supposed to be moved? But I've also seen it on a van making deliveries for an office supply store; the van had four wheels, so I know that was a mistake.
"I'm no expert on bears, but I think we should remain stationary."

An *anecdote* is a short, amusing story relating a true incident.
"That was a cute anecdote, Ed. So did you ever find the snake?"

An *antidote* is a chemical used to counteract the effects of poison.
"That was a cute anecdote, Ed. Now please get me the antidote!"

☐ Use *hardy* to describe something that has strength or endurance.
"What a hardy plant. I haven't watered it in three years."

☐ Use *hearty* to describe abundance, enthusiasm, or a nutritious food.
"The ad promised a hearty sandwich for hearty appetites. I ate four."

☐ To *imply* means to say something without directly stating it.
"What are you implying, Detective? You think I blew up the bank?"

☐ To *infer* means to conclude or suppose, based on information.
"I infer from your lawyer's letter that you're unhappy with my work."

Remember, use *imply* to send out information, and *infer* to draw it in.

☐ *Compliment* means to say something nice.
"That's your seventh piece of cake. I'll take that as a compliment."

Complimentary means free of charge.
"This vegetable chopper comes with a complimentary first aid kit."

☐ *Complement* means to make complete.
"Betty, this seaweed wine complements the candied snails perfectly."

Complementary means suitably paired, often producing completeness.
"No, your purple shirt doesn't match the lavender pants, but they're still complementary and, I think, quite stylish."

☐ *Advise* is a verb. It means to help someone by making suggestions.
"Gus, for your own safety, I'd advise you to stop hanging from there."

☐ *Advice* is a noun. It refers to the suggestion itself.
"You took my advice and it got you fired? Oh. Sorry about that."

☐ *Lend* is a verb. You lend someone money, or a rake.
"Dad, would you lend me twenty dollars so I can pay Mom back?"

☐ *Loan* is a noun. You go to the bank for a loan.
"What? You took a loan from somebody named Crazy Frank?"

Writing Rules!

☐ *Discreet* means appropriately restrained or tactful.
"I know you love Grandma's jewelry, but be discreet; she's still alive."

Discrete means separate or distinct.
"His speech is so soft and rushed, it's hard to identify discrete words."

☐ *Disinterested* means impartial, unbiased, not taking sides.
"The judge was disinterested and fair; I guess I wasted that $50 bribe."

Uninterested means bored, distracted, inattentive, apathetic.
"The class was uninterested in the math lecture; many played poker."

☐ *Sank* is the past tense of sink.
"My heart sank when I saw what he'd done to my hair."

Shrank is the past tense of shrink.
"I shrank my mother's favorite sweater, so I hid it in my shirt pocket."

☐ *Prescribe* means to order or dictate.
"The law prescribes that you stop at red lights, Dan. Try to remember."

Proscribe means to prohibit.
"Isn't there some rule that proscribes him from parking that army tank on his front lawn?"

☐ *Adverse* means difficult or contrary.
"I'm afraid the tornado will create adverse conditions for badminton."

Averse means resistant or unwilling.
"He was averse to fighting, and so had little success as a boxer."

☐ Use *that* to identify a specific individual among a group.
"The books that are on this shelf are all in Danish."

Use *which* to give some extra information about something.
"I'll have the apple danish, which is my favorite dessert."

☐ *Anxious* means filled with anxiety -- nervous, fearful, worried.
"You seem anxious, Al. Don't worry. Cliff diving is completely safe."
"Ben had been anxious about that test, and sure enough, he got a 12."

☐ *Eager* means filled with anticipation or motivation.
"After six months on the space station, the astronauts were eager to visit a convenience store, and a real bathroom."
"Rachel and her husband had different opinions about the ballet; she was eager to go, while he hoped for four flat tires."

☐ *Accept* is a verb. It means to receive or allow. The noun is *acceptance*.
"I accept your apology, Martha. Now please get your car off my foot."
"We hope Greg gets accepted to college so we can rent out his room."

☐ *Except* is usually used as a preposition and indicates exclusion. It can also be a conjunction, meaning unless or only. The noun is *exception*.
"Everyone is invited to the self-esteem celebration, Tom, except you."
"I play tennis every day, except when it's too hot, too cold, too cloudy, too windy, a weekend, a holiday, my birthday, or if I need a haircut."

☐ *Pique* means to arouse, annoy, or stimulate. *Peek* means to take a quick look. *Peak* is the top of something, such as a mountain, a cloud, or a swirl of whipped cream. The following sentence uses all three. It's pretty pathetic and is presented here only for the sake of clarity. Try not to write like this:

"Our sense of wonder was piqued when we reached the mountain peak just as the sun began its first peek through the ghostly mist."

☐ A *tenet* is a principle or belief.
"Crustaceanism is an unusual religion; its main tenet is the belief in a giant, all-knowing lobster."

☐ A *tenant* is someone who pays rent to occupy a space.
"We evicted our tenant after we found out he was breeding panthers in his apartment. His lease clearly states, No Pets."

☐ *Consists of*, *composed of*, and *comprises* are all used when explaining some whole thing and what its parts are. If you want to be grammatically correct (especially on a standardized test), use them this way:

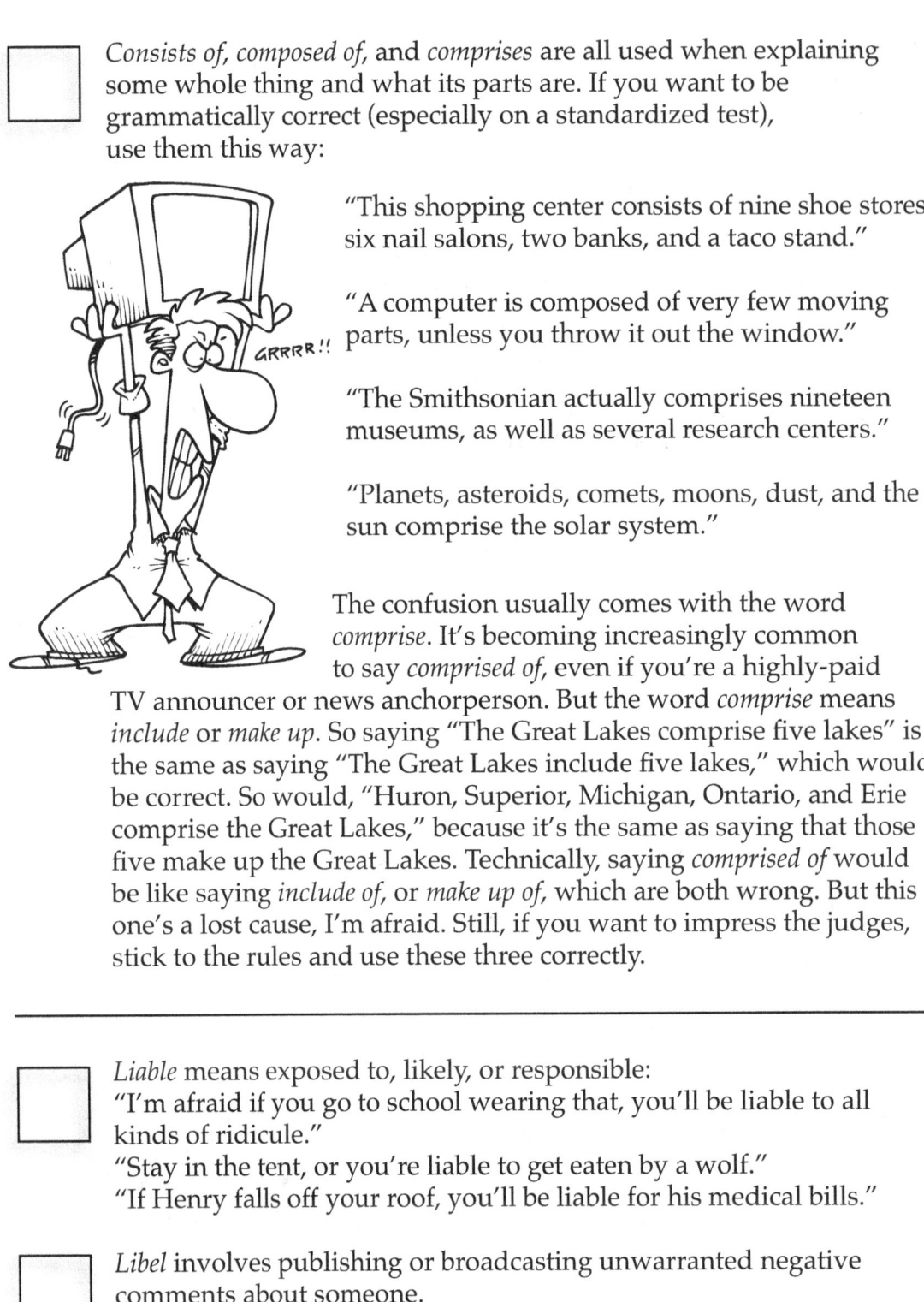

"This shopping center consists of nine shoe stores, six nail salons, two banks, and a taco stand."

"A computer is composed of very few moving parts, unless you throw it out the window."

"The Smithsonian actually comprises nineteen museums, as well as several research centers."

"Planets, asteroids, comets, moons, dust, and the sun comprise the solar system."

The confusion usually comes with the word *comprise*. It's becoming increasingly common to say *comprised of*, even if you're a highly-paid TV announcer or news anchorperson. But the word *comprise* means *include* or *make up*. So saying "The Great Lakes comprise five lakes" is the same as saying "The Great Lakes include five lakes," which would be correct. So would, "Huron, Superior, Michigan, Ontario, and Erie comprise the Great Lakes," because it's the same as saying that those five make up the Great Lakes. Technically, saying *comprised of* would be like saying *include of*, or *make up of*, which are both wrong. But this one's a lost cause, I'm afraid. Still, if you want to impress the judges, stick to the rules and use these three correctly.

☐ *Liable* means exposed to, likely, or responsible:
"I'm afraid if you go to school wearing that, you'll be liable to all kinds of ridicule."
"Stay in the tent, or you're liable to get eaten by a wolf."
"If Henry falls off your roof, you'll be liable for his medical bills."

☐ *Libel* involves publishing or broadcasting unwarranted negative comments about someone.
"The article you wrote about me is libelous, and you'll be hearing from my attorney, Mom."

☐ *Pore* as a verb means to study or read carefully.
"We pored over his letters, hoping to understand his sudden obsession with wool slippers."

☐ *Pour* is a verb, too, but it means to dispense a liquid, or a flow of some kind.
"As she poured the milk over her corn flakes, she also poured out her heart to me. It was pretty messy."

☐ *Wet* means to add moisture.
"I could tell the towel was wet, and knew immediately that someone had taken a bath."

☐ *Whet* means to stimulate, excite, or sharpen.
"The movie did whet my desire for a good mystery, but I fell asleep in my popcorn and missed the ending."

☐ *Pare* means to cut away or reduce.
"We had to pare down the budget, Russ. So we're selling your desk and chair."

☐ *Pair* means two of something. *Pear* is a fruit.
"Look, Ethel. There's a pair of sandals hanging from the pear tree."

☐ *Site* refers to the location of something.
"This was once the site of the world's first convenience store."

☐ *Sight* has several meanings, including a thing or place that can be seen or visited (often confused with *site*).
"We saw all the usual sights in San Francisco, as well as a few that were unusual."

☐ *Waive* means to give up something, such as a right.
"My client has waived his right to a last meal, your honor, but wonders if he could catch the end of the game."

☐ *Wave* refers to a swinging motion, or a sudden abundance.
"Overcome by a wave of fear, he waved a white flag to surrender."

☐ *Bated* means reduced in intensity. It's related to the verb *abate*, and is most often used to describe breath that is shallow or held completely.
"She waited with bated breath as the winner of the Miss Bermuda Triangle pageant was announced."

☐ *Baited* means lured, as with bait or a decoy.
"We baited the thief with money, jewelry, and peanut M&Ms."

☐ *Marshal* is a verb and means to gather, arrange, or assemble.
"Marshal all of our armies and meet me back here in five minutes."

☐ *Martial* is an adjective; it comes from Mars, the Roman god of war, and refers to anything related to fighting.
"I am a master of all of the martial arts, so you'd better back down. I'm serious."

☐ A *council* is a group of people who discuss issues and make decisions.
"We submitted a request to the council, but they told us to buzz off."

☐ To *counsel* means to give advice.
"I'm not qualified to counsel you legally, but I think you should return the statue to the park."

☐ *Elude* means to escape or evade.
"He eluded the police by disguising himself as a moose."

☐ *Allude* means to refer to something indirectly; suggest or imply.
"If you're alluding to that time I painted your car, I said I'm sorry."

☐ *Incite* is a verb and means to arouse or inflame; pronounced in-SITE.
"Your public protests nearly incited a riot, and worse, tied up traffic for hours."

☐ *Insight* is a noun and means a clear and deep understanding of a complex problem; pronounced IN-site.
"Your insight, Harry, into the challenges facing cucumber farmers is quite touching."

Dumber & Dumbest

☐ **Comparative adjectives.** A comparative compares two things and identifies which of the pair has *more* of some quality.

"Let's see who's **faster**, Mario or that German Shepherd."
"Sandy is **funnier** than her sister, but not in a good way."
"Phobos is the **larger** of Mars's two moons, and has a **smaller** orbit."

☐ **Superlative adjectives.** A superlative compares three or more things and identifies which of the group has the *most* of some quality.

"They're the **toughest** team in the league, and that's why I hate them."
"John is the **tallest** person in this class picture. He's the one whose head is cut off."
"I've been to all nineteen bakeries in the city, and this one is the **best**."

As & Like

☐ Most often, the mistake here is the use of *like* when *as* is needed. *Like* is correct when you're comparing two things; it should follow a verb and should be followed by a noun, pronoun, or gerund.

"My landlord looks **like a pair of old boots**."
"I'm sorry, I just didn't expect ice cream to taste **like that**."
"Do you feel **like hang-gliding** today, Grandpa?"

☐ *As*, *as though*, and *as if* should be followed by a subject and verb:

"**As we said** earlier, we have no interest in selling the windmill."
"You sound **as though you're planning** to go back to Uganda."
"He walks around here **as if he just discovered** the New World."

Writing Rules! 27

Redundancy

If you say the same thing more than once, or in more than one way, it may be annoying to your reader, who has laundry to do and hamsters to feed and doesn't want to waste time plowing through your endlessly-repetitive prose. Here are a couple of habits to avoid.

☐ *Reason why*
The word *reason* already contains the idea of *why*, so there's no need to put them together. Saying *reason why* is like saying *cold ice* or *hot fire* or *sweet sugar*. Some people compound the problem by adding *because*: "The reason why I cut down your peach tree is because I wanted to try out my new power saw." These people should be imprisoned with no possibility of parole. Shorter and simpler is better:

"The reason I cut down your tree is that it was infected with a South American fungus."
"I cut down your tree because I'm allergic to peaches."
"Oh, was that your tree?"

☐ *Both at the same time*
Some words are just unnecessary. "Carl and Roger both tried to kick each other." Do you see that the word *both* isn't needed? It wouldn't be possible for just one of them to try to kick each other, so saying *both* and *each other* is redundant. Same with this: "Now Carl and Roger are both apologizing at the same time." This makes more sense: "Carl and Roger tried to kick each other. Now they're both apologizing."

☐ *When* or *whenever*?
The word *whenever* should be used if you're talking about something that happens repeatedly, or over a long period of time. (Don't use *whenever* with *always* -- that would be redundant.)
"I get heartburn whenever my Aunt Roberta comes over."
"Whenever I clean the couch, the cat throws up on it."

Use *when* if the event is infrequent or uncertain.
"We ran into our neighbors when we were on vacation in Bolivia."
"When you get to the waterfall, turn right."

☐ *Where is it at?*
Does deleting the word *at* change the meaning of the sentence?
No? Then you don't need it.

☐ *Over* or *over top*?
I've never understood this one. *Over* means over. Why would you need to add the word *top*? You'd never say *under bottom*. It's similar to *reason why*. Too many words. Here, these sound all right to me:

"Just spread the rest of that frosting over the cake, and then get out of my way."

"The sundae had chocolate sauce on top, and a cherry on top of that. But I'm not really thinking about it at all."

"We applied a second coat of stain over the entire floor, and that's when the bag of flour fell off the counter."

☐ *Free gift*?
We've been hearing about free gifts for so long from people trying to sell us something, we've forgotten how redundant the phrase is. A gift, by definition, has to be free -- otherwise, it isn't a gift.

"Order the complete set of twelve nail-clippers in the next fifteen minutes, and we'll send you this toothbrush warmer free. If not completely satisfied, simply return the nail-clippers for a full refund, and keep the toothbrush warmer as our gift."

☐ *Very unique*?
How unique can something be? The word *unique* means it's the only one. The sun is unique in the solar system. The Empire State Building is unique. So is the Great Wall of China.

"Beth, your decorating style is unique. I've never seen so many coffee tables in one room."

☐ *At 5 a.m. this morning...*
I hear this on the news all the time. When you say *a.m.*, there's no need to add *morning*. Another redundant time: *12 noon*. Noon is enough.

☐ *Freezing cold*?
I can't explain it, but *boiling hot* sounds descriptive to me. *Freezing cold* just sounds redundant.

Writing Rules!

One Word or Two?

☐ *alright* or *all right*
If you look in the dictionary, *alright* is there, but it still bugs me. I was taught it's *all right*, so alright looks alwrong. The original confusion probably came from *already*, which is a word. But it's not the same as all ready, is it? *Already* means so soon, as in "You're here already? We weren't expecting you until November." *All ready* has a completely different meaning: "The kids are all ready to go, and we're just waiting for my husband to finish trimming his beard."

"The salsa tasted all right, but the expiration date was last March."
"Is it all right with you if I sleep on the lawn?"

☐ *a lot*
Again, two words. If you write *alot*, you should be willing to write *alittle*. (I believe this is another lost cause, but I'm hanging on anyway, old geezer that I am.)

"Eleven dollars? That seems like a lot of money for a coloring book.
"It was a four-hour movie, so we ate a lot of Milk Duds."
"I like you a lot, Marshall, but I just lost everything in the mudslide, and my pet crocodile needs a root canal."

☐ *no one*
Always two words.
"I'm telling you, Ashley, there's no one under your bed. Besides, monsters always hide in the closet. Good night, Sweetie."

☐ *anywhere, nobody, nowhere, someone, somewhere, sometime, somehow*
One word.

a while or *awhile*
Either is correct.

☐ *anyways, anywheres, somewheres, hisself*
These are not words! They may very well be in the dictionary. I don't know and I don't care. Writing them will make you sound uneducated, so don't do it!

Writing Rules!

☐ *anytime* or *any time*
It depends. As an adverb, it's one word:
"Come back anytime, Cliff, but wear a shirt from now on."

But sometimes *any* is an adjective and *time* is a noun, so they should be separate:
"Do you have any time to look at pictures of our trip to Wisconsin?"

☐ *getaway* or *get away*
Again, it depends. There's a poster at my bank that says, "You deserve to getaway." Or something like that. Anyway, it bothers me every time I see it. *Getaway* is usually a noun: "That was a relaxing getaway, and now I'm ready to get back to the screwdriver factory." It can also be an adjective: "He stole the bubblegum machine and she drove the getaway car."

But when you need a verb ("Get away from me or I'll tell the warden"), use two words. It's the same with *castaway*, a person or thing that has been lost or discarded. ("The dazed castaway washed up on the deserted beach with a sudden craving for root beer.") But sometimes it needs to be a verb: "You're going to cast away our entire marriage to go save some frogs?" Same with *may be* and *maybe*: "I may be way off base here and maybe you are telling the truth, but I think you're the one who picked all my tomatoes."

☐ *altogether* or *all together*
Altogether is an adverb that means entirely or to the full extent.
"He had me altogether convinced he was an astronaut."

All together means in a group, or all at once.
"They've put my favorite national anthems all together on one CD!"

☐ *takeoff* or *take off*
This is the same as *getaway*. *Takeoff* is a noun, an event:
"What a bumpy takeoff! Hey, isn't that our luggage on the runway?"

Take off is a verb, an action:
"Joel, please take off your grandfather's World War I uniform."

Odds & Ends

☐ *Okay*, not *O.K.*
An abbreviation in the middle of a sentence interrupts the flow of your writing. Give each word the space it deserves.
"Okay, okay, I'll take my biology project out of the refrigerator. Relax."

☐ *Would have*, not *would of*
This is an example of writing exactly what you hear, but what you're hearing is distorted.
These are correct:
"I would have washed the dishes, but I'm still eating."
"You could have borrowed the money yesterday, but it's a new day."
"We should have realized those goats couldn't swim."

☐ *Numbers*
When do you use numerals and when do you use the number word? I usually spell out a number if it's a hundred or smaller. There are exceptions, of course. If it's the grade on a test or the temperature or a price, it might make more sense to go with the numerals. Be consistent: don't use numerals, then switch to words, especially if you're going for dramatic effect:
"We left Las Vegas, where it was 115 degrees, and six hours later landed in Alaska, where it was 42."

☐ Avoid stretching out short words for emphasis. It doesn't work, seems childish, and can completely destroy the mood you've created:
"We were sooooooo glad to be released by our kidnappers."

☐ Never use email or text messaging terminology in an essay. It's *because* (not cuz), *you* (not U), *are* (not R), and so on. And please don't abbreviate entire phrases. LOL is the single most annoying thing I have ever read. (So far.)

☐ Refrain from using strings of exclamation points or question marks. If you need punctuation to suggest emotions such as excitement or puzzlement, your words are weak.

"Wow, Tommy, where did you get the cool motorcycle????? My brother had one just like it!!!! And wait, it like disappeared just the other day!?!?!?"

☐ Watch your spelling on certain words with several syllables and repeating letters. Have you ever written *rembered*, when you meant *remembered*? Or *thermeter* when you intended *thermometer*? Mortifying, isn't it? Also, the word is *adaptation*, not *adaption*.

☐ A sentence that starts with *I wonder* or *I wanted to ask you* is a statement and doesn't need a question mark at the end:

"Nancy, I wonder if you'd like to attend the Dry Cleaners' Masquerade Dance with me."

"Mr. Costello, I wanted to ask you if you'd consider raising my grade from a D to a B-plus."

Notice the distinction between these two:

"I was just sitting here asking myself why I left the sunroof open when I knew there was a blizzard coming."

"I was just sitting here asking myself, "Why did you leave the sunroof open when you knew there was a blizzard coming?"

☐ *A Few Things Not To Do:*

Don't write *these ones* and *those ones*. Don't say them either. In fact, just to be safe, don't even think them.

Don't refer to people with the word *that*. Use *that* when you're talking about a lamp or a skateboard or a beef burrito. For people, use *who*. "This morning at the clinic, I examined a woman who had an extra set of fingernails."

Don't say or write *irregardless*; the word is *regardless*.

Don't write *um*. Ever. Ever.
"Um, Mr. President, I think I forgot to mention that you were scheduled to have breakfast with the prime minister of Romania this morning."

☐ *Supposedly* or *supposably*?
I was ready to tell you not to use *supposably* because it isn't a word. But when I looked it up, there it was. Who knew?

What Are You Talking About?
(That sentence needs a subject, and related problems.)

We're not going to get into the many complexities of sentence structure. I know you're disappointed, but we just don't have the space. For that you need one of those massive 800-page slabs with titles like *Mastering the Fundamentals of Essential English Grammar and Punctuation, Fourth Edition*. Here, we're going to keep it simple. Most sentences are saying that something has happened, is happening, or will happen. Answer the question "Who or what is causing it to happen?" and you've snared yourself a subject. The action of the sentence is called the predicate; the predicate is (or contains) a verb. The recipient of the action is the object. We often use little squiggles, called punctuation, to help clarify the meaning of the sentence. And there you have it: *Mastering the Fundamentals of Essential English Grammar and Punctuation in One Paragraph, First Edition*.

Here are a few examples, just in case you missed something.

"Marvin has driven his minivan into the canal."
What event is this sentence describing? A minivan being driven into the canal. Who? Who drove the minivan into the canal? Marvin did, so he is the subject. What is the predicate? *Has driven his minivan* (containing the verb *has driven*). And *into the canal* is called a prepositional phrase. Because the sentence has a subject and a predicate, presents a complete thought, and contains adequate punctuation, it's a complete sentence. These are also complete sentences, with subjects in bold:

"**You** should turn off your scooter when inside the library."
"**Melissa** just sank a twenty-foot putt."
"**This bottle of ketchup** exploded inside my refrigerator."

Now it's also possible that Marvin has driven his minivan into the canal and yet somehow has avoided being the subject of the sentence. The following sentences, again, have the subjects in bold:

"**The minivan** was driven into the canal by Marvin."
"After finishing her Sudoku, **Paulette** noticed that Marvin had driven his minivan into the canal."
"**The expired inspection sticker** seemed to interest the police more than the fact that Marvin had driven his minivan into the canal."

☐ The following are not complete sentences, because they lack either a subject or predicate; they're called **fragments**. Used correctly (and sparingly), they can spice up your writing. Really. When they appear in a question on any standardized test of writing and grammar, however, they will always represent mistakes that need to be fixed.

"Wandering through the streets of Minneapolis."
(No subject -- who is wandering?)

"The boy with raisin-colored eyes and a shy smile."
(No predicate -- what's the boy doing?)

"Just over the next hill."
(No subject or predicate -- who's doing what over the next hill?)

Now let's complicate things a little:

"Melissa just sank a twenty-foot putt and I didn't have my camera."

☐ This is a **compound sentence**. It has two complete sentences connected by the conjunction *and*. We know they're both complete sentences because each has a subject (*Melissa* and *I*) and a predicate (*just sank* and *didn't have*). But watch what happens when we remove the *and*:

"Melissa just sank a twenty-foot putt I didn't have my camera."

☐ We have a **run-on sentence**. Each part is perfectly clear, but it's too much information for one sentence. (True, we have no trouble understanding the meaning, but that's not the point. Rules are rules. Think of it as food. You have a bowl of spaghetti for dinner. Then you have a piece of cheesecake for dessert. Each is delicious, and each is a welcome part of your meal. But put them together on the same plate and not so good. A run-on sentence, then, is like spaghetti cheesecake.)

Here are a few more run-on sentences:

"The powerful hurricane whipped through the town nearly every house was damaged."
"Baseball is a warm weather sport playing it in the cold seems odd."
"Your whistling is starting to bug me please cut it out I mean it."

Writing Rules! 35

As with fragments, run-on sentences can be used creatively. For example, if you're describing a fast-paced scene or a confusing dream, they can help the reader get a feel for your subject and the pace of the action. But if you're going to use them, the rest of your writing has to be so impeccable that the reader has no doubt that you included the run-on sentences on purpose. In a college application or standardized test essay, it's not worth the risk. Be creative, but in ways that are grammatically correct.

> Remember, on a grammar test, a run-on sentence is ALWAYS wrong. There are several things you can do to make it right.

1. Break the run-on into two shorter sentences, separated by a period.
"My mother gave me a haircut to save money now we have to buy a hat."
"My mother gave me a haircut to save <u>money. Now</u> we have to buy a hat."

2. Keep the run-on as one sentence, but insert a conjunction.
"Alfred told me it was safe to park the car on the frozen lake he was mistaken."
"Alfred told me it was safe to park the car on the frozen lake, <u>but</u> he was mistaken."

3. Separate the run-on phrases with a semicolon.
"He was wearing brand new sneakers everyone could hear him squeaking down the hallway."
"He was wearing brand new <u>sneakers; everyone</u> could hear him squeaking down the hallway."

The period gives a stronger break. I'd recommend using it when the two sentences are separate thoughts, even if they're closely related, as in number 1 above. Use a conjunction when the two phrases combine to make a single point, as in number 2. In a similar way, separate the phrases with a semicolon when you want to give your reader a brief rest, but also want to make it clear that the two ideas go together. In example 3 above, the two parts don't seem to give enough information to justify separate sentences. Here, see for yourself:

"He was wearing brand new sneakers. Everyone could hear him squeaking down the hallway."

Get it? Okay. That's all I'll say about run-on sentences.

I changed my mind. Here's some more about run-on sentences. I know I said we were done, but the problem is so prevalent, I have this nagging feeling that you don't completely get it. If I'm wrong, feel free to skip this page and move on.

You're probably tired of this run-on business. I know. You've been hearing this since third grade. But you have to understand it and make the necessary changes. There are natural pauses in writing, just as there are in speech. Have you ever listened to someone who doesn't stop talking long enough to breathe? The words just come pouring out in a flood, and you eventually get tired and your mind wanders. Soon you're thinking of ways to get away. You may even consider resorting to some act of physical violence. (Believe it or not, there are people who are that picky about grammar. Can you imagine?)

☐ Here's still another example of a run-on sentence, followed by several ways to fix it. (Technically, this one is called a **comma splice**, because it has independent clauses separated by commas. But it's really the same problem: too much talking, not enough breathing.)

"I walked out to the barn, my horse Billy was eating a grilled cheese sandwich, that's his favorite snack."

That sentence has three subjects (*I*, *my horse Billy*, and *that*) all fighting for attention. Here are a few better ways to write it:

"I walked out to the barn and found my horse, Billy, eating a grilled cheese sandwich; that's his favorite snack."

"I walked out to the barn. My horse, Billy, was eating his favorite snack: a grilled cheese sandwich."

"I walked out to the barn. My horse, Billy, was eating a grilled cheese sandwich, which is his favorite snack."

"I walked out to the barn. My horse, Billy, told me to get lost and not come back without his grilled cheese sandwich."

It's Right Because It's Right
(Which also means it's wrong because it's wrong.)

The English language has some logic built into it, but not much. There are many things we say just because that's the way we say them. It's called correct **usage**. For example: "We'll be dining on pizza and mashed potatoes this evening." See that preposition *on*? There's no logical reason for saying *on* in that context. We don't literally mean we'll be on the food, any more than we mean speak *up* or tune *in*. We just have certain ways of saying things. You're familiar with many. Here are a few you may be a little fuzzy about:

preoccupied with:
"Are you preoccupied with something? You haven't touched your turnips."

oblivious to (or *of*)
"Connie slept on the beach, apparently oblivious of the incoming tide."

different from (or *than*)
"Riding a unicycle isn't different from riding a bicycle, except for the pain."

in contrast to (or *with*)
"In contrast to his campaign speeches, the new mayor seems to be in favor of bribery and corruption."

from a to b
"Tomorrow's quiz will be on all pages from 8 to 644."

between a and b
"They promised to deliver the bed sometime between 8 a.m. and October."

Don't write: "We're open from 9-6." Better: "We're open from 9 to 6." Or, "We're open 9-6."

☐ The word *repeated* should be used to refer only to occurrences after the first one. In other words, if Billy falls off his tricycle, and then has the same accident a second and third time, he repeated it twice. (It happened three times, but was repeated two.)

☐ Use *any other* when comparing someone or something to all others. "Einstein was smarter than any other scientist in the world."

You can't logically say that Einstein was smarter than any scientist, because then he'd have to be smarter than himself, and that's really hard, even for Einstein.

Just Between You and Me
Pronouns, Prepositions, and Objects

There are subject pronouns and there are object pronouns. The subject pronouns are the ones that perform some action -- they are the doers in the sentence. The object pronouns are the receivers of the action. Whatever is happening in the sentence, it's happening to them.

Subject Pronouns
I you he she we they who it

Object Pronouns
me you him her us them whom it

So we say, "He hit me with a bag of doughnuts." We don't say, "Him hit I with a bag of doughnuts." (Unless the doughnuts were really stale and caused some kind of head injury.)

Now there are these other things called **prepositions**. You've no doubt heard of them. Here are a few common prepositions:

at, of, to, for, through, over, under, behind, with, around, between, on, against, about, near, before, after... and there are many more.

Prepositions link nouns and pronouns with the rest of the sentence. The thing they link to is called the object of the preposition, and that will usually be a noun or an object pronoun. In each of the following sentences, the preposition is in *italic* and the object of the preposition appears in **bold**:

"As a comet gets *near* **the sun**, its tail seems to trail *behind* **it**."
"The comments were clearly meant *for* **us**."
"Pam sent invitations *to* **Fred, Manny, and me**."
"Why did you throw that shovel *at* **him**?"
"*Between* **you and me**, I doubt he'll show up."
"Would you rather sit *next to* **her**?"
"He's going to the prom *with* **whom**?"
"See those penguins crossing the road? Try to drive *around* **them**."

Writing Rules!

There are several special cases that cause more than their share of trouble. The most common is when a pronoun follows some form of the verb *to be*.

Let's say you knock on someone's door (someone who's expecting you) and they say, "Who is it?" You could answer, "It's me!" and get away with it, because that's usually how we talk. But to be technically correct, you should say, "It is I." Just as when someone calls on the telephone and asks for you, the correct response would be, "This is she," or "This is he."

For some reason, the phone response doesn't sound nearly as awkward and pretentious as announcing, "It is I!" at the door. But traditional English grammar calls for the subject pronoun in that situation, because the verb isn't suggesting an action, but rather a state of being. If you want to sound less stuffy, or avoid causing people to roll their eyes, just say, "It's Bobby Joe!" or "It's your dearest friend!" or "I can't remember. I fell and hit my head. I was hoping you'd know who I am."

While we're on that subject, rewriting a sentence is often easier than trying to make an awkward phrase work. Sometimes we paint ourselves into a corner, then go looking for a smart person to help us get out of it. The trick is to avoid the corner in the first place. Here's an example:

"Linda felt that the two best players on the team were Val and she."

It's grammatically correct, but this would be less clumsy:

"Linda felt that she and Val were the two best players on the team."

Here are a few more pairs of sentences. In each case, the second version is better (in my opinion):

"The story you're telling has already been heard by Tammy and me."
"Tammy and I have already heard this story."

"The person answering the telephone should identify himself or herself."
"When answering the telephone, be sure to identify yourself."

"Basketball is a hard game to master, which we haven't done yet."
"We'll probably never master the game of basketball."

"In case you're wondering, the sender of the letter was I."
"In case you're wondering, I sent the letter."

A Lesson from the Mailbox
The dreaded participial phrase

"As a valued Cardmember, I am pleased to bring you this special opportunity..."

That was the opening line in a letter I recently received from the vice president of marketing at a major credit card company. The letter made me happy for several reasons. Mostly, the low interest rate allowed me to bury myself even more deeply under the mammoth mountain of debt I'd been accumulating since my twenties. But it was also a sparkling example of bad grammar, one that I could use to help you learn a little something. On top of that, I hoped you'd find encouragement in the fact that it's possible to boot the language around and still make a lot of money. (I assume that the VP makes a decent salary based on his ability to snare the high rollers, and despite his trouble with sentence structure.)

Okay. Let's get to work. What's wrong with that sentence up there?

First, look at the first four words, followed by the comma. That's called an introductory participial (*par-tuh-SIP-ee-ul*) phrase, a group of words that describes or modifies the subject. You're probably thinking, so what? And I'd have to agree with you. But don't miss the point. That participial phrase is supposed to be talking about the subject of the sentence. Just who is the valued cardmember here, anyway? It's not the VP. It's the person getting the letter. So here's how it has to work: the first word *after* the comma should be the person being described in the phrase *before* the comma. These two would be correct:

"As a valued Cardmember, you are receiving this offer because..."
"As a highly-paid vice president of marketing, I am honored to send you this offer..."

See? The way it was originally worded, the writer was setting up one joke, then giving the punchline to another. It can cause confusion. In this case, I knew what he meant. But take a look at this sentence:

"As the person who received the most votes in the election, I'm calling to congratulate you on your victory."

Do you see how the speaker switches tracks in mid-sentence? The first word after the comma should be *you*.

"As the person who received the most votes in the election, you should be proud of your shocking victory." Or, "As the person who received the most votes in the election, I'm calling to rub it in that you lost! Again!"

There's another, less glaring, error in the original sentence. It's the word *bring*. You bring something from there to here. You *take* or *send* something from here to there. (See page 17 for more about this.) The VP wasn't bringing the offer; he was sending it. That's it. I won't pick on him anymore. (Wait, one more thing. Why is the word *Cardholder* capitalized? Okay, that's really it this time.)

Here are sentences that contain participial phrases. The ones in **bold** are correct. Pay enough attention to these phrases and they'll begin to jump out at you, even when you're not looking for them. Won't that be fun?

"Scratching furiously, I knew my dog was being tormented by fleas."
"Scratching furiously, my dog seemed to be tormented by fleas."

"Waving from the field below, the pilot could see the trapped campers as they tried to catch his attention."
"Waving from the field below, the trapped campers tried to catch the pilot's attention."

"As your dentist, you have to know how concerned I am about the sheer volume of blood that's gushing from that back molar."
"As your dentist, I'm somewhat concerned about the sheer volume of blood that's gushing from that back molar."

"Racing out of control, I could see the fire quickly devour the village."
"Racing out of control, the fire quickly devoured the village."

Try to hear the participial phrase as it announces itself. Then quickly determine whom or what the phrase is describing: Who is scratching furiously? Who is waving from the field below? Who is the dentist? And who or what is racing out of control? The answers to those questions should appear immediately after the comma.

Can We Reach An Agreement?
Subjects and Verbs

This is a big one. The bad news is that questions on subject-verb agreement appear on almost every standardized writing test. More bad news: this is a common source of trouble; ask three people for writing samples and you'll probably see two mistakes related to subject-verb agreement. The good news is that you already know the rules; if you listen carefully, you can usually hear the difference between right and wrong. Consider the following sentences.

"The twelve <u>books</u> of Latin grammar I borrowed from the library <u>are</u> all due back today. So <u>is</u> the <u>set</u> of classical music CDs. May I borrow the car keys, Mom?"

The subject of the first sentence is plural (*the twelve books*), so the verb *are* is needed. In the second sentence, the subject is *set*, and requires the singular verb *is*. There are many such words that represent more than one person or thing, but are, in fact, singular: set, group, collection, team, class, family, audience, department, committee, squad, troop, flock, herd, and so on; all need singular verbs.

"Our <u>class</u> <u>is</u> going on a field trip to the dry cleaner."
"That <u>herd</u> of elephants <u>seems</u> to be moving this way."
"Where did Ted say his priceless <u>collection</u> of stamps <u>was</u>?"

Okay, here's one of the problem areas. When words such as *either, neither, anyone, someone, everyone, no one,* and *each* are used, they require a singular verb:

"<u>Either Tim or Carlton</u> <u>is</u> going to win the taco-eating contest."
"<u>Neither Tim nor Carlton</u> <u>appears</u> to want any dessert."
"Would <u>anyone</u> like to give up <u>his</u> seat?"
"<u>Everyone</u> <u>has</u> an equal chance to win this contest."
"<u>No one</u> <u>is</u> going to show up for your Fourth of July Eve Party."
"<u>Each</u> of you <u>is</u> welcome to make a stunningly-large donation."

The special case of *there is*:
"There is a rhinoceros in the dugout and three giraffes in centerfield." In this sentence, there are two subjects (*rhinoceros* and *three giraffes*). The verb is determined by the first subject. Rhinoceros is singular, so the verb *is* must be singular, as well.

☐ In almost all other situations in which there are two or more subjects, the verb agrees with the subject it's closest to. So:

"Either Georgina or her <u>two sisters</u> <u>are</u> going to ride in the back seat."

"Neither the team members nor the <u>coach</u> <u>wants</u> to lose this game."

☐ Confusion most often arises when a long group of words comes between the subject and verb. We sometimes try to get the verb to agree with one of the words in that long group, as in the following examples. The correct subjects and verbs are underlined.

"<u>Martha</u>, after consulting with her doctors, parents, best friends, and several complete strangers she met at the car wash, <u>is</u> going to move forward with the eyebrow transplant."

"The entire <u>family</u>, along with several close friends, <u>is</u> trying to plan a reunion in the Caribbean."

But:

"The entire <u>family and several close friends</u> <u>are</u> trying to plan a reunion in the Caribbean."

☐ One more case: the **subjunctive**. This sounds scary, I know. You use the subjunctive form of verbs all the time, but just aren't aware of it. (That's no reason to be afraid. You're probably using your spleen right now, and I bet that doesn't scare you.) The subjunctive is needed when expressing a wish, or describing a situation that doesn't exist. In the following pairs of sentences, the ones in **bold** are correct.

"Pam wishes her apple tree was producing more fruit."
"Pam wishes her apple tree <u>were</u> producing more fruit."

"If it was up to me, we'd buy the bulldozer."
"If it <u>were</u> up to me, we'd buy the bulldozer."

"He spends money as if he has an endless supply."
"He spends money as if he <u>had</u> an endless supply."

This is the lost cause in this category: the use of *here's* and *there's* with plural subjects. I hear it everywhere. I read it on the front pages of newspapers. I see it in magazines and books. "Here's seven things you must do to lose weight!" "There's ten reasons to visit Albania now!" "Here's the answers to your questions!" "There's many ways to reach your goals!"

☐ The correct versions, of course, would say either *here are* or *there are*. One exception, I think, would be a reference to money. "There <u>is</u> thirty dollars in her savings account" seems correct, because it's describing a total amount. If you were talking about the *number* of dollar coins in a jar, then you could say, "There are thirty dollars in this jar."

A Few More Things to Stop Doing

☐ *snuck*. The past tense of *sneak*? It's grown in acceptance over the years, but it's still a mistake on standardized tests. The correct form is *sneaked*. "Bernard sneaked into the garden and ate our cucumbers."

☐ *us being able to*. This phrase and others like it call for the possessive. "She couldn't close that door without **our** being able to hear it." "I appreciate **your** wanting to help." "We were surprised by **his** trying to swim across that lake."

☐ *as best as I could*. Such an awkward phrase, and you can sometimes watch people trapping themselves with it while speaking. It's easy to fix: "I did the best I could." Or, "I did as well as I could."

Redundancy. Again.

☐ *new addition*. "We're building a new addition onto our house." No, you're not. You're building an addition. Of course it's new. That's what an addition is.

☐ *revert back*. The word *revert* means to go back, so *revert back* is redundant. "Harold, you seem to be reverting to your old ways. Please give me back my sandwich."

☐ *connect together*. The word *together* is unnecessary. "We needed to connect three extension cords in order to plug in the electric wheelbarrow I got for my birthday."

Verb Tenses

The difficulty with verb tenses is usually not a matter of confusing past, present, and future. Your ear is reliable enough to handle those, along with the Continuous version of each:

Present
"I eat fish for breakfast."

Present Continuous
"We are filling the pool with banana pudding."

Past
"She begged her mother to unlock the window."

Past Continuous
"Bill was mowing the lawn when the hickory tree fell."

Future
"You will spend the rest of your life in prison, I fear."

Future Continuous
"They will be returning tomorrow, so let's lock the doors."

The problems arise when you have to deal with the so-called perfect tenses. Why are they called perfect tenses? I have no idea. But their use can be confusing, especially on the SAT and other standardized tests that tend to use long, wandering sentences for you to figure out. Here's an example:

"In 1974, President Richard Nixon was caught in the trap of his own secret system of tape recordings, and has resigned from office."

The problem with this sentence is the switch from past tense (*was caught*) to present perfect (*has resigned*). The past tense verb indicates that the action was completed a long time ago. But the present tense suggests a recent development. They don't work together. The sentence might have made sense in the early months of 1975, but not for very long. Here are two improvements:

"In 1974, President Richard Nixon was caught in the trap of his own secret system of tape recordings and resigned from office."

Better: "Caught in the trap of his own secret system of tape recordings, President Richard Nixon resigned from office in 1974."

The perfect tenses you should know are: Present Perfect, Present Perfect Continuous, Past Perfect, Past Perfect Continuous, Future Perfect, and Future Perfect Continuous. They sound scary. They're not.

Present Perfect
Use this tense when you're talking about something that happened (or did not happen), and you want to take it right up to the present moment. However, the timeframe is not clear. (You would say, "I have been to that store," but not "I have been to that store last Thursday.") More examples:

"She has not seen her cousin in a long time."
"Have you ever worn a gorilla costume?"
"Despite his well-groomed appearance, Dan has never taken a bath."

Present Perfect Continuous
Use this tense when you're talking about something that has been happening for some time -- and is still going on. Examples:

"Do you realize you've been talking non-stop for six hours?"
"Beth has been living in that house since Hoover was president."
"They have been waiting at the wrong airport all day."

Past Perfect
This tense is used to described something that happened in the past and is now over; it also explains that the event described took place before some other event. It sounds confusing, but examples should help clear it up:

"We had already eaten lunch by the time Sid arrived."
"Had you ever heard the cow speak before yesterday, Miss Marsh?"
"He looked as though he had begun to cut his own hair, then changed his mind about halfway through."

Past Perfect Continuous
Describes an ongoing action in the past, immediately followed or interrupted by some other event.

"He denied it, but I'm sure Phil had been sleeping when I called."
"The birds had been living in the attic for years before we arrived."
"We had been planning to visit Aunt Emma this summer, but I guess now it's too late."

Writing Rules!

Future Perfect
This tense designates some future event that will be completed before some other event occurs. It usually contains the phrase *will have*, followed by the past tense of a verb.

"By September, we will have built our first home-made helicopter."
"Jimmy will have eaten both apple pies before his father wakes up."
"I will have been out of high school for forty years by the time my son graduates."

Future Perfect Continuous
Describes a future action that is still taking place when some other event occurs.

"You will have been making payments for twenty years by the time you own the house."
"When the submarine surfaces, they will have been living on board for five months."
"By the time spring arrives, I will have been training for a year."

Many people seem to have trouble remembering the simple past tense of several verbs. This is illustrated by the fact that standardized tests almost always include at least one sentence containing these errors:

sang, not *sung*
"We sang all night, or at least until the police arrived."

sank, not *sunk*
"I'm telling you, Malcolm, our boat sank in the lake. See? Gone!"

shrank, not *shrunk*
"Uncle Fred, either I grew or you shrank since last Christmas."

When considering whether a verb tense is grammatically correct, always assume the sentence was written recently. For example:

"Nineteenth-century factory workers will enjoy the benefits of workplace reform." If this sentence had been taken from a late eighteenth-century or early nineteenth-century newspaper article, the future tense (*will enjoy*) would be grammatically correct. But presented as part of a test question, such as one you might find on the SAT, you would be expected to change the verb to the past tense (*enjoyed*).

Infinitive or *-ing* Verb?

Wait! What's an infinitive? It's just a verb with the word *to* in front of it: to drink, to fly, to pretend. The infinitive form is always used after certain verbs, such as *want* or *promise*; the list of those verbs would be much too long to present here, but a few examples should help:

"I want to join you on your mission to Pluto. I'm already packed."
"Rhonda has promised to feed the dogs during our trip to Peru."
"He expects to hear soon that he's set the new hiccup record."

Can you see that it would be difficult to construct those sentences with *-ing* verbs? "Rhonda has promised feeding the dogs..." People whose first language is not English sometimes make such errors in speech. Not a big problem, and you can understand the intended meaning with little effort. But make the same mistakes on a standardized test and you'll lose points.

There are other times, of course, when *-ing* verbs are the only kind that'll work. If someone asks you what you're doing, you almost have to answer with an *-ing* verb:

"Hey, Gus, what are you doing in the closet?"
"I'm looking for my Papa Smurf hat."
"I'm hiding from my father. He saw the dent in the car."
"I'm testing out my new night-vision goggles."

Here's an exception:
"I'm trapped between the coats. Get help!"

Just to add a little more confusion, there are these things called **gerunds**. They look like *-ing* verbs, but they're used as nouns or adjectives. In some cases the gerund is required, while in others the infinitive is needed. And sometimes, it's okay to use either. Here are examples of each:

"I enjoy sleeping on a bed of small metal screws." (gerund)
"She's trying to knit a sweater, I think." (infinitive)
"They like climbing trees." (gerund)
"They like to climb trees." (infinitive)

A gerund can serve as the subject:
"Snacking is my favorite thing to do, after eating."

...or the object:
"Wendy despises dancing and won't leave her chair."

Grammar is a Parallel Universe

Here's a rule that's guaranteed to be on any standardized test of written English. It's called *parallel structure*, or *parallelism*, and while it may sound like a rule for building a porch, it's all about grammar. If you've done a fair amount of reading, you're already sensitive to writing that violates it.

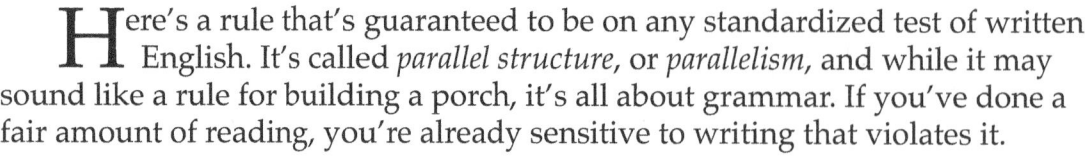Parallelism is simply a pattern within a sentence. Following the rule is a matter of maintaining the pattern once you've established it.

"Bailey's hobbies include fishing, hiking, and mountain-climbing."

Do you see that there are three items listed in that sentence, and that all three are in the same form? That's parallel structure. Here's one way that sentence could have been written **incorrectly**:

"Bailey's hobbies include fishing, hiking, and to climb mountains."

You know from reading the previous page that the above sentence has two gerunds and an infinitive. Bad structure. The original sentence had three gerunds. Good structure. Another example:

"The manager's plan for improving the team included hiring a pitching coach, scheduling regular practices, and comfortable uniforms."

Again, the pattern is broken: *hiring, scheduling,* and where's that third *-ing* verb? There are several ways to fix it.

"The manager's plan for improving the team included hiring a pitching coach, scheduling regular practices, and designing comfortable uniforms."

Or, "The manager's plan for improving the team included a pitching coach, regular practices, and comfortable uniforms."

So far we've looked at sentences that had items listed, and we've tried to make sure the items followed a pattern. But parallelism goes beyond lists of words. Entire phrases should also exhibit parallelism.
In the following example, matching phrases from the first and second halves of the sentence appear **bold**, *italic*, and <u>underlined</u>.

"**Cal planned** *to attend meetings in the morning* <u>and then relax for the rest of the day</u>, while **Al chose** *to sleep until noon* <u>and then go to the later sessions</u>."

Writing Rules!

It's easy to miss less-glaring examples of unparallel structure, especially on the SAT or some other mind-numbing, time-pressured test. Here are a few you could easily fly right past.

"Taylor couldn't decide between her friend's wedding and taking that free trip to Puerto Rico."

On first or second reading, the sentence may seem fine the way it is. But consider the parallel structure here:

"Taylor couldn't decide between <u>her friend's wedding</u> and <u>that free trip to Puerto Rico</u>."

Or, "Taylor couldn't decide between <u>attending her friend's wedding</u> and <u>taking that free trip to Puerto Rico</u>."

Another:

"Please indicate whether you'd prefer steak or lamb, cooked medium or well-done, with a serving of potato or you can substitute rice."

Again, it seems all right, and certainly if you were hearing that sentence from a waiter or waitress, you would be focused on the food choices and not the grammar. But as a piece of writing, it lacks parallel structure. Better:

"Please indicate whether you'd prefer steak or lamb, <u>cooked</u> medium or well-done, <u>served</u> with potato or rice."

Another:

"The person we hire for this position must be honest, motivated, and someone we can rely on."

Notice that the list contains two adjectives (*honest* and *motivated*), then suddenly introduces a phrase with no adjective (*someone we can rely on*) as the third item. Here's the same sentence with parallelism. Note that now, the list contains three adjectives:

"The person we hire for this position must be honest, motivated, and reliable."

Putting Modifiers in Their Place

Another picky rule that doesn't seem to make sense. If a sentence flows naturally, why mess with it, especially if the meaning was clear all along? Because, as in so many other situations, the rules are stricter in formal writing than they are in casual writing or speech. Consider this sentence:

"The governor announced that she would only discuss the main parts of the new budget."

Seems clear. But if you interpret it to mean that out of the many parts of the new budget, the governor would be discussing just the main ones, then the modifier *only* is misplaced. According to the strictest grammar experts (and they're the ones we should listen to when preparing for any writing test or assignment), the modifier must be placed closest to the word or phrase it's intended to modify. In this case, that would be *main parts*:

"The governor announced that she would discuss <u>only the main parts</u> of the new budget."

If we move the modifier around, we change the meaning of the sentence. Look:

"<u>Only the governor</u> announced that she would discuss the main parts of the new budget." This means the governor made the announcement by herself, without any staff accompanying her.

"The governor <u>only announced</u> that she would discuss the main parts of the new budget." She only announced it; she didn't elaborate, explain, defend, or take questions.

"The governor announced that <u>only she</u> would discuss the main parts of the new budget." She would be the only person discussing the main parts of the budget.

"The governor announced that she would discuss the main parts of <u>only the new budget</u>." Back to the original version of the sentence. She would be talking about the new budget, but would not discuss any of the old budgets.

Writing Rules!

Don't Change Your Voice!
(Who's speaking and who's listening?)

"<u>You</u> shouldn't eat hair gel, no matter how hungry <u>you</u> feel."
"<u>We</u> are going back to the hotel to change <u>our</u> socks."
"<u>One</u> is compelled to warn one's neighbor of approaching lava."
"<u>I</u> want to make it clear that <u>I</u> don't even own an umbrella."

Notice that, in each of the above sentences, the relationship between writer and reader stays consistent. Depending on the subject matter and the purpose of the writing, one type of relationship may be more effective than another. For example, addressing the reader as *you* can help create a casual tone, while the use of the pronoun *one* sounds more formal.

The key, though, is consistency. This is another rule that will <u>always</u> appear in at least one question on standardized writing tests. Learn to automatically look for it, especially when you see either the word *you* or *one* in a sentence. (If you see both, that's probably the problem.) Here are a couple of examples that contain errors; in each sentence, the words that should match are in **bold**.

"**One** needs to think quickly if **you** want to avoid a falling piano."
"When **I** look closely at the evidence, **we** can see that Barry is guilty."
"If **one** is honest with **himself**, **he** will see that cauliflower is not edible."

Neither-Nor, Either-Or

Still another one. The word *neither* has to be matched with the word *nor*, and *either* has to be matched with *or*. You cannot mix them, and if you see them mixed in a sentence on a test, jump on it, because that's the error. Here are a few examples of these words used correctly:

"<u>Either</u> Morris <u>or</u> Sal is going to be my new barber."

"Either would be a fine choice."

"<u>Neither</u> Morris <u>nor</u> Sal knows anything about cutting hair."

"Neither one will give you a decent haircut. I'd try Mr. Pompadouris down the street."

Writing Rules!

The Elusive Semicolon

We talked about semicolons a bit in the section on run-on sentences, and maybe it was enough. Or maybe you already felt warm and cozy with the semicolon long before you ever picked up this book. If so, move on. But I know there are people out there who are still confused by this annoying little piece of punctuation. This page is for them.

First, the name, *semicolon*. It doesn't make sense. It sounds like something you'd find in a medical textbook. And the mark itself is also strange. A colon is two dots. A semicolon should be one dot.

So what's it for?

☐ A semicolon replaces the period between two sentences when those sentences are so closely related that they really convey one idea. *But there must be a complete sentence on each side of the semicolon.* Here are two sentences that <u>should</u> be separate:

"Ronald was puzzled by the humming sound coming from the top of the tall oak on his front lawn. Across town, Ronald's father sat in the banquet room of a lavish hotel and prepared to explore yet another business opportunity."

Those two sentences are complete, and seemingly unrelated. They have been correctly kept apart by a period. But consider these two:

"As Ronald struggled to see through the tree's dark upper branches, he had a sudden urge to flee; at that moment, miles away, his father was struck by the same feeling."

They could have been written as separate sentences. But as one, they work together to show you that Ronald and his father were sharing the same reaction to different events. The sentences could also be connected by the conjunction *and*, but the semicolon provides a more dramatic pause.

In the following example, the semicolon does the opposite: it helps you understand that the action has two parts, but that they are very nearly simultaneous. There's a cause-and-effect, but they almost overlap.

"Gerard opened the washing machine and pulled out his new red sweater, followed by his wife's underwear and white pants, all now a frightening shade of pink; he felt himself leave his body, as if he were having a near-death experience right there in the laundry room."

Ifs, Ands, & Buts
Using the right conjunction.

A conjunction is a word, usually a small one, that connects other words or phrases within a sentence. There are all kinds of conjunctions linking all kinds of phrases, but it gets complicated, and even if I thought I could explain it, you'd only get mad and stop reading halfway through. So let's keep it simple and focus on these two: coordinating conjunctions and subordinating conjunctions.

☐ A **coordinating conjunction** connects words, phrases, or independent clauses. (An independent clause is part of a sentence that could be a complete sentence all by itself.) The conjunctions are in **bold**:

"My two favorite sports are baseball **and** daydreaming."
"Venus is a planet, **but** Pluto is now just a dog."
"He has just eaten an entire box of Twinkies, **yet** he hungers still."
"Angelo shares with students his love of writing **and** his passion for art."

☐ A **subordinating conjunction** begins a dependent clause. (A dependent clause is not a sentence because it doesn't express a complete idea; rather, it is a phrase that in some way supports an independent clause.) In each of the following sentences, the subordinating conjunction and its dependent clause are in **bold**, with the conjunction also underlined. The rest of the sentence is an independent clause.

"**<u>Although</u> hail the size of apples fell from the sky all day**, Nicholas continued to paint the fence."

"I have decided not to attend that college, **<u>because</u> I didn't get accepted**."

"**<u>If</u> that rabid hyena rings the doorbell again**, don't answer it."

On a standardized test such as the SAT, a grammar question concerning conjunctions will often gauge your ability to use *and* and *but* correctly:

"We had been told of his brilliantly insightful wit, <u>and</u> his performance was dull and shallow."

The phrases *brilliantly insightful wit* and *dull and shallow* indicate a result that contradicted the expectation. So the sentence needs the conjunction <u>but</u>. Substitute it for the underlined <u>and</u> in the original sentence and it should make more sense. There are many more of these questions in the next section.

Hopefully, An Answer to the Adverb Question

Sadly, there are way too many adverbs floating around. Tragically, many people sap the energy from their writing by misusing them, and personally, I believe it's a serious problem. Thankfully, there is hope. And happily, you've found it.

Does that first paragraph sound lame, but acceptable? Well, it is, and it isn't. All of those sentences contain adverbs (ending in *-ly*) that are used in ways that diminish their power. They sound all right when spoken, and they're fine for informal writing, but when it comes to living up to their true potential, they let the reader down. Honestly, they do.

An adverb modifies a verb. You remember. So it describes *how* something is being done.

"He walked **slowly**, hindered by the air conditioner strapped to his back."

"I waited **nervously** as my dentist rummaged through his toolbox."

"Brent moved **effortlessly** through the water, his foot caught in a rope attached to the back of a speeding boat."

An adverb should help you picture the action. She doesn't just shake her head; she shakes it **furiously**. Or **timidly**. Or **confidently**. Now re-read the heading at the top of this page and the sentences in that first paragraph. Can you picture the action being modified by the adverbs *hopefully, sadly, tragically, personally, thankfully,* and *happily*? I can't. It's like biting into cotton candy. The harder I try, the more quickly it disappears. Same with the word *honestly* at the end of the second paragraph. The only verb in that sentence is *do*. But is something being done honestly? No, and I say that honestly.

Do those adverbs have any place? Can they be used correctly? Yes:

"We listened hopefully, thinking the judge might change her mind."
"'My goldfish just exploded,' Joan said sadly."
"Their lives ended tragically when the lighthouse fell down."
"I delivered it personally, not trusting the post office or anyone else."
"Paul answered thankfully, relieved that he would soon be rescued."
"My daughter giggles happily whenever I trip over something."

Seriously, when dealing with adverbs in an essay or on a test, is it hard to avoid slipping into informal and even sloppy usage? Apparently.

The word *bad* is an adjective, and should be used that way.
The word *badly* is an adverb.

Some people feel strongly about grammar, while many others couldn't care less. But if you go online and do a search of these two words, you'll discover that this one touches a nerve. I've never understood what the controversy is about (and I've tried). Here is the issue in a single sentence:

"I feel badly about running over your ferret, Jim."

Badly? Why badly? You'd never say, "I feel happily" or "I feel angrily," would you? You would say, "I feel good about my sweater selection." Or "I feel nervous about staying at that underwater hotel." Or "I feel frustrated about this year's turnip crop." In each case, we used an adjective (*good*, *nervous*, *frustrated*) to describe our feelings (an adjective describes a noun, and an adverb describes a verb). Why, then, do some people insist on changing the rule in this one case? I think *badly* should be used to described how skillfully (or unskillfully) a person does something: "Wow, I have to say, Mike performed badly in the chainsaw competition."

Through frequent (though mistaken) usage, the words *bad* and *badly* are becoming interchangeable. But my advice would be to stay consistent: I feel happy, I feel confident, I feel bad.

Wait a minute! Look, right up there. It says, "Some people feel strongly about grammar." *Strongly*. Did I contradict myself before I even started? No, I don't think so. To say someone feels strongly is to describe the intensity of their feelings. It's illustrating *how* they're feeling, not *what* they're feeling. It isn't the same as saying that someone feels strong. Here, look:

"Popeye felt strongly that we should eat our spinach."

"Popeye felt strong after he ate his spinach."

Wow, a whole page on *bad* and *badly*. I'm going to end it here, before you get the idea that we've touched a nerve or something. Because we haven't. Seriously, I don't even care.

Writing Rules!

The Mysterious *They*

☐ Here's something to avoid in your writing, and keep in mind when answering grammar questions. When you're using a pronoun, always be sure it refers to a previous noun, and that it's clear which noun. The most common violation is the word *they*.

"I read the newspaper this morning, and they said the world is going to end next Tuesday."

This could be an important piece of information, depending on who *they* are. If they're scientists, I'd probably want to know more. If they're a religious cult or someone trying to sell books or a movie, leave me alone, I have a refrigerator that needs cleaning. Meanwhile another example:

"Those little stuffed bears were so expensive a few years ago, and now they can't even give them away."

As a spoken statement, perfectly clear. As a written sentence, not so good. Again, who are they? A pronoun is standing in for a noun, and it should be obvious to the reader which noun. In that last example, the only two nouns are *bears* and *years*. This would be better:

"Those little stuffed bears were so expensive a few years ago, and now collectors can't even give them away."

☐ Sometimes the problem is too many nouns. If you're going to use a pronoun to refer to one of them, be clear. Imagine getting this message in your inbox:

"Hey, I was talking to Shelley, Sheryl, Shannon, Shania, and Sharlene a little while ago, and she wants to give you some money. But you have to call her within the next ten minutes."

Wouldn't that be annoying? Unless you had them all on speed-dial. These are just confusing:

"Karl's pet monkey died while he was on vacation in Denmark."
"The fortune-teller told Tammy where to find the treasure, and now she's a wealthy woman."
"Sam knew the hungry cat had spotted the chicken sandwich, but he ate it anyway."

A Lesson from Another Writing Guide
Possessive + Gerund

**"Keep It Simple, Stupid.
(Please don't be offended by us calling you stupid.)"**

The two sentences above appear in a writing workbook published by a large, well-known, and successful tutoring company. There's no need to explain what the passage was about, beyond the idea that simple writing is better than fancy, complex, hard-to-understand writing. The point is, the word *us* is a mistake.

Calling in that sentence is a gerund, a concept you may remember from an earlier page. The word *us* was intended to modify the gerund. We usually need to use a possessive in that situation. The sentence should read:

"Please don't be offended by <u>our</u> calling you stupid."

Will this rule appear as a question on a standardized test? Very likely. So here are a few more examples of gerunds correctly modified by possessives.

"I must object to <u>your</u> yelling out insults during the funeral."
"Harry seemed surprised by <u>our</u> landing the hot air balloon on his deck."
"She grew tired of <u>Ted's</u> dressing up in circus costumes at home."
"Brian hated his <u>son's</u> quitting the lacrosse team."

The key is to figure out what the sentence is trying to say. In the last example above, did Brian hate the son or the quitting? If it was the son, rewrite the sentence like this: "Brian hated his son, especially after the boy quit the lacrosse team." But more likely, the original sentence was trying to say that Brian hated the fact that his son had quit the team. For that, we need possessive plus gerund, and the sentence was correct as written.

Here's an example that probably wouldn't require the possessive:

"I was shocked to see <u>Mike</u> eating at the next table in the diner."

The shock was seeing Mike, not the fact that he was eating at a diner. That's what people do at diners. So there's no need to modify the gerund.

Note: The use of examples from letters or other publications does not suggest that this book is free of errors. In fact, it's highly probable that this book is *riddled* with mistakes. It's just easier to make fun of other people.

Writing Rules!

Practice Questions
Part 1: Finding the Error

If you're going to take the SAT or some other standardized test that features questions related to writing and grammar, do as many practice questions as you can. You'll quickly see that there's a lot of repetition. You won't necessarily see the exact same sentences, but you will see the same types of sentences. For example, there will *always* be questions involving incorrect verb tenses, subject-verb agreement, parallel structure, and so on. As you do more and more practice tests, you'll find yourself knowing the answer to many questions as soon as you start to read the sentence. You'll spot the word *neither* and immediately look for its partner, *nor*. You'll see the word *one* used in the third-person narrative voice and suspect a switch to the second-person *you* -- and sure enough, there it'll be.

This is not to suggest that you should rush through the questions, or fail to read the sentences completely. Don't jump to conclusions. Slow down and make sure. But also trust your ear for the language. Read the sentence silently, but hear it in your mind. If something sounds wrong, it probably is.

One more thing. The sentences on these tests tend to be long, cluttered with all kinds of words, phrases, and punctuation. They also have underlined parts, which can be distracting. The errors are often far apart, separated by the clutter. This may be an obstacle at first, but it too will soon lose its power as you learn to recognize each question type and the likely answer.

For each of the following sentences, identify the grammar or usage error it contains. The letter corresponding to the mistake is the answer to that question. If a sentence has no error, its answer is E.

Answers and explanations begin on page 67.

1. Design patents for the stapler, a standard fixture in modern offices (A) and classrooms, was awarded to (B) (C) several different people on both sides of the Atlantic in the (D) mid-1860s. No error (E)

2. It seems clear that, in this age (A) of free agency and huge contracts, loyalty to a team or its fans is often (B) (C) outweighed by an athlete's desire of earning more money. No error (D) (E)

3. The <u>creation</u> of an attractive and
         A
   <u>healthy garden</u> requires planning
         B
   the layout, gathering <u>useful</u>
                           C
   information, removing weeds,
   and <u>to water and fertilize</u> when
          D
   necessary. <u>No error</u>
              E

4. Many people say <u>they would</u>
                        A
   <u>welcome the opportunity</u> to travel
            B
   into space, but <u>how many</u> would be
                       C
   willing <u>to endure</u> the training and
              D
   risks involved? <u>No error</u>
                      E

5. The commuter train <u>rushed past</u>
                          A
   Andrea and <u>I</u> so quickly that we
              B
   barely had time <u>to look up</u> from our
                       C
   magazines <u>and</u> see it go by.
              D
   <u>No error</u>
      E

6. <u>Since</u> we <u>have become</u> so
      A   B
   dependent on computers and other
   electronic devices that we almost
   <u>lose our ability</u> to function <u>when</u>
         C   D
   they're not working. <u>No error</u>
                           E

7. Mark, Ellen, and Roger <u>are</u> all
                             A
   powerful debaters, <u>but</u> I'd have to
                         B
   <u>say that</u> Ellen is the <u>stronger</u> of the
       C   D
   three. <u>No error</u>
              E

8. As instant replay becomes more
   <u>widely used</u> <u>in professional sports</u>,
        A   B
   the decisions <u>that were getting</u>
                      C
   made by umpires, referees, and
   other officials may begin to carry
   <u>less weight</u>. <u>No error</u>
        D   E

Writing Rules! 61

9. Modern television has given
                  A
us an unprecedented look into the
                     B
lives of people scarred by violence,
                C
caught in scandal, and charged with
                                D
criminal activity. No error
                   E

10. In 1875, Matthew Webb earned
                            A
worldwide fame and adulation
                    B
when he swum across the English
         C
Channel, becoming the first person
known to have accomplished the
       D
feat. No error
      E

11. If one is going to master any
              A
art form, including music, dance,
          B
painting, photography, or any of
          C
the others, you have to be prepared
            D
to learn and practice the necessary
skills. No error
       E

12. We're accustomed to our vans
          A
and SUVs, and are, for the most
part, unaware that our vehicles
      B   C
tend to be bigger than most other
                 D
countries. No error
           E

13. An economic downturn can be a
                          A
time of opportunity it forces people
        B
to think of innovative ways to
   C
generate income, and often pushes
                        D
them onto a completely new career
path. No error
      E

14. Walking through the state park
on a moonless and foggy night,
even the slightest sound caused
        A
me to stop and look around in
   B   C
anticipation of some imminent
              D
calamity. No error
          E

15. Every day, firefighters <u>all over</u>
                              A
the world <u>bravely rush into</u> burning
          B
buildings to save people, pets, and
property, <u>irregardless</u> of the dangers
          C
<u>involved</u>. <u>No error</u>
    D   E

16. <u>Driven by instinct</u> and <u>their</u>
        A   B
collective push to survive as a
<u>species, penguins</u> endure frigid
    C
temperatures and months without
food in order <u>to care for</u> their
              D
unhatched eggs. <u>No error</u>
                      E

17. Everyone <u>attending</u> the lecture
                  A
knew that the speaker, a <u>renowned</u>
                          B
archeologist, <u>had been</u> blind since
              C
birth, <u>so it wasn't</u> surprising to hear
       D
her describe shades of color with
such precision. <u>No error</u>
                     E

18. <u>It may be</u> more fun to think
        A
an unusual light in the night sky
<u>could of been</u> a craft from another
    B
solar system, but there <u>is</u> no
                        C
credible evidence our planet
<u>has been</u> visited by extraterrestrials.
    D
<u>No error</u>
    E

19. <u>When</u> the Soviet empire
        A
collapsed in the early 1990s,
<u>there</u> <u>wasn't hardly</u> a nation that
   B   C
remained <u>unaffected</u>. <u>No error</u>
             D   E

20. We wondered <u>who's</u> tools those
                      A
<u>were</u> on the beach, because we
   B
<u>had set</u> sail with the belief that we
    C
<u>would be</u> the first humans to ever
    D
set foot on the island. <u>No error</u>
                            E

21. At some point <u>during</u> the weeks
               A
and days before the Civil War, it

<u>became clear</u> to both sides that
      B

neither compromise <u>or</u> the abolition
                    C

of slavery <u>would</u> preserve the union
            D

without bloodshed. <u>No error</u>
                       E

22. It's difficult <u>for</u> a company
                    A

<u>to maintain</u> high productivity
      B

when <u>they keep</u> <u>issuing</u> new and
       C   D

contradictory objectives. <u>No error</u>
                              E

23. <u>Identifying</u> the world's tallest
      A

statue isn't as easy <u>as you</u> might
                       B

expect, <u>but</u> it seems clear that
          C

the winner is one of several

representations of Buddha,

<u>located</u> in China, Japan, Thailand,
  D

Myanmar, or Taiwan. <u>No error</u>
                        E

24. I heard the storeowner say he

<u>was open</u> for business from ten
   A

in the morning <u>and</u> eight in the
                 B

evening, <u>yet</u> when I arrived just
           C

after noon, the doors <u>were</u> locked.
                         D

<u>No error</u>
   E

25. Few <u>promises made</u> during a
          A

political campaign <u>are</u> as <u>likely</u> to
                    B   C

win votes <u>than</u> those concerning the
            D

reduction of taxes. <u>No error</u>
                        E

26. My brother and <u>me</u>, always
                    A

competitive <u>with each other</u> in
              B

school and on the basketball court,

<u>learned</u> to cooperate after inheriting
  C

and expanding our <u>parents'</u> family
                    D

business. <u>No error</u>
              E

27. Despite the wild dreams of a
    A
few engineers, there's no plans to
              B
build a tunnel under the Atlantic
    C
Ocean, from the east coast of the
    D
United States to the west coast of

Europe. No error
         E

28. In 1893, New Zealand became
                            A
the first nation in which women
                 B
were gaining the right to vote.
    C   D
No error
    E

29. Although Emily Dickinson

wrote more than 1,800 poems, yet
  A   B
only seven were published during
              C   D
her lifetime. No error
              E

30. A living cell is like a tiny
                    A
city, with systems in place for
       B   C
transportation, energy production,

repairs, and waste disposal.
                    D
No error
    E

31. Weatherwise, we would rely on
    A   B
the forecast to help us make daily
                             C
plans, only to arrive at the beach in
            D
the middle of a thunderstorm.

No error
    E

32. Every detail of the surprise
                 A
party were carefully planned, but
      B   C
somehow Kim, whose birthday we

were celebrating, arrived before

most of the guests did. No error
    D   E

33. In the early 1800s, Napoleon

Bonaparte declared himself emperor
           A
of France and then conquered
                B
most of Europe, but was unable to
                     C
maintain his stranglehold on the

nation of Haiti that same year.
                 D
No error
    E

Writing Rules! 65

34. It was neither the heat nor the
                                A
mosquitoes that made the concert so

unpleasant, but rather the amount
            B   C
of people packed into such a small
         D
space. No error
        E

35. I was surprised by you arriving
     A   B
so early for the meeting; it allowed
        C
us to finish right on time. No error
   D   E

36. Anne proved to be an excellent
            A
counselor, as much for her ability
           B
to listen and encourage as for her
                        C
incite into the problems of early
 D
adulthood. No error
            E

37. Light travels at 186,000
         A
miles per second in a vacuum,

but slows down when
 B   C
moving through any
 D
other medium. No error
               E

38. A parent often faces the

dilemma of having to choose
          A
between what will make the child

happy for the moment or what will
      B   C
be best for the child in the long run.
                      D
No error
E

39. Fuji is not only Japan's tallest
                                A
mountain, and is also a dormant
          B
volcano considered sacred by the
        C   D
nation's Buddhists. No error
                     E

40. With the electoral votes divided

between four candidates in the
  A
presidential election of 1824, the

House of Representatives chose
                           B
John Quincy Adams as the

victor, even though Andrew
        C
Jackson had won the
        D
popular vote.

No error
E

Writing Rules!

Answers to Practice Questions, Part 1

1. (B) The subject, *design patents*, is plural and requires the verb *were*.

   Design patents for the stapler, a standard fixture in modern offices and classrooms, **were** awarded to several different people on both sides of the Atlantic in the mid-1860s.

2. (D) If *desire* is followed by a verb, it's usually the infinitive form.

   It seems clear that, in this age of free agency and huge contracts, loyalty to a team or its fans is often outweighed by an athlete's desire **to earn** more money.

3. (D) The three *-ing* verbs follow parallel structure; so should the fourth.

   The creation of an attractive and healthy garden requires planning the layout, gathering useful information, removing weeds, and **watering and fertilizing** when necessary.

4. (E) No error.

5. (B) The preposition *past* needs an object pronoun.

   The commuter train rushed past Andrea and **me** so quickly that we barely had time to look up from our magazines and see it go by.

6. (A) *Since* shouldn't be used as a substitute for *because*. Here, it's unnecessary.

   We have become so dependent on computers and other electronic devices that we almost lose our ability to function when they're not working.

7. (D) When comparing three or more, use the superlative.

   Mark, Ellen, and Roger are all powerful debaters, but I'd have to say that Ellen is the **strongest** of the three.

8. (C) The phrase *that were getting* is awkward and unnecessary.

   As instant replay becomes more widely used in professional sports, the decisions **made** by umpires, referees, and other officials...

9. (E) No error.

10. (C) The past tense of *swim* is *swam*.

    In 1875, Matthew Webb earned worldwide fame and adulation when he **swam** across the English Channel, becoming the first person known to have accomplished the feat.

11. (D) The sentence starts out using third-person (*one*), then switches to second-person (*you*).

    If one is going to master any art form, including music, dance, painting, photography, or any of the others, **one must** be prepared to learn and practice the necessary skills.

12. (D) When making comparisons, be sure to compare like objects. This sentence sounds as though our vehicles are bigger than countries.

    We're accustomed to our vans and SUVs, and are, for the most part, unaware that our vehicles tend to be bigger **than those of most** other countries.

13. (B) Run-on sentence. Here's one way to fix it:

    An economic downturn can be a time of **opportunity; it** forces people to think of innovative ways to generate income, and often pushes them onto a completely new career path.

14. (A) The subject should follow the participial phrase.

    Walking through the state park on a moonless and foggy night, **I found that even the slightest sound** caused me to stop and look around in anticipation of some imminent calamity.

15. (C) *Irregardless* is not a word.

    Every day, firefighters all over the world bravely rush into burning buildings to save people, pets, and property, **regardless** of the dangers involved.

16. (E) No error.

17. (D) The second half of the sentence presents an illogical conclusion.

    Everyone attending the lecture knew that the speaker, a renowned archeologist, had been blind since birth, so it **was** surprising to hear her describe shades of color with such precision.

18. (B) *Could have been* or *could be*.

    It may be more fun to think that unusual light in the night sky **could have** been a craft from another solar system, but there is no credible evidence our planet has been visited by extraterrestrials.

19. (C) *Wasn't hardly* is a double negative.

    When the Soviet empire collapsed in the early 1990s, there **was hardly** a nation that remained unaffected.

20. (A) Wrong word.

   We wondered **whose** tools those were on the beach, because we had set sail with the belief that we would be the first humans to ever set foot on the island.

21. (C) Match *neither* with *nor*.

   At some point during the weeks and days before the Civil War, it became clear to both sides that **neither** compromise **nor** the abolition of slavery would preserve the union without bloodshed.

22. (C) *Company* is singular; should be *its*. Avoid unclear pronouns.

   It's difficult for a company to maintain high productivity when **it** keeps issuing new and contradictory objectives.

23. (E) No error.

24. (B) *From... until.*

   I heard the storeowner say he was open for business **from** ten in the morning **until** eight in the evening, yet when I arrived just after noon, the doors were locked.

25. (D) *As likely... as.*

   Few promises made during a political campaign are **as likely** to win votes **as** those concerning the reduction of taxes.

26. (A) Needs subject pronoun, *I*.

   My brother and I, always competitive with each other in school and on the basketball court, learned to cooperate after inheriting and expanding our parents' family business.

27. (B) Subject-verb agreement (plural).

   Despite the wild dreams of a few engineers, **there are no plans** to build a tunnel under the Atlantic Ocean, from the east coast of the United States to the west coast of Europe.

28. (C) *Became* is past tense; second verb should match.

   In 1893, New Zealand became the first nation in which women **gained** the right to vote.

29. (B) *Although* and *yet* serve the same purpose; use one or the other, not both.

   Although Emily Dickinson wrote more than 1,800 poems, only seven were published during her lifetime.

30. (E) No error.

31. (A) Putting *wise* at the end of a noun is lazy writing. Avoid it if you can.

We would rely on the **weather forecast** to help us make daily plans, only to arrive at the beach in the middle of a thunderstorm.

32. (B) Subject-verb agreement (singular).

Every **detail** of the surprise party **was** carefully planned, but somehow Kim, whose birthday we were celebrating, arrived before most of the guests did.

33. (D) *That same year* is unclear. What year? Either delete it or give the date.

In the early 1800s, Napoleon Bonaparte declared himself emperor of France and then conquered most of Europe, but was unable to maintain his stranglehold on the nation of Haiti.

34. (C) Use *amount* for cole slaw or gravel, but *number* for people.

It was neither the heat nor the mosquitoes that made the concert so unpleasant, but rather the **number** of people packed into such a small space.

35. (B) That gerund (*arriving*) needs a possessive modifier.

I was surprised by **your** arriving so early for the meeting...

36. (D) Wrong word.

Anne proved to be an excellent counselor, as much for her ability to listen and encourage as for her **insight** into the problems of early adulthood.

37. (E) No error.

38. (C) *Between... and*

A parent often faces the dilemma of having to choose **between** what will make the child happy for the moment **and** what will be best for the child in the long run.

39. (B) *Not only... but*

Fuji is **not only** Japan's tallest mountain, **but** is also a dormant volcano considered sacred by the nation's Buddhists.

40. (A) Use *among* with three or more.

With the electoral votes divided **among four** candidates in the...

Practice Questions
Part 2: Fixing the Error

This section presents sentences with just one part underlined. In most cases, this underlined phrase has a problem, and you have to find the answer that fixes the problem. As in the previous section, a few of the sentences are fine, but in that case the answer is A, which simply repeats the underlined part of the sentence.

Try to hear yourself reading each answer choice in your mind. Very often, incorrect answers will be obvious. Most sound awkward. And again, if it sounds bad, it probably is.

The original sentence usually has a minor error, similar in a way to a small ketchup drip on your pants. You know how, when you try to wipe off the drip, it just spreads the stain and makes a big mess? Most of the answer choices in this type of question are like that, so you can eliminate them immediately. Answers that switch to a passive verb are wrong. If something can be said clearly in fewer words, that's almost always better. Run-on sentences and sentence fragments are always wrong, as are unclear pronouns, inconsistent verb tenses, and lack of parallelism. Sometimes a sentence might sound okay, but one of the answers makes it better; don't choose too quickly.

Okay, enough gabbing. Let's do a few. Answers and their explanations start on page 77.

41. Samantha thought back to the first day of seventh grade, and realized that was <u>the time when her problems began</u>.

(A) the time when her problems began
(B) the time at which her problems began
(C) the time when her problems had begun
(D) when her problems began
(E) when her problems got their beginning

42. Laughing out loud at the joke his brother had told him earlier, <u>it suddenly dawned on Lou that he was at a seance</u>.

(A) it suddenly dawned on Lou that he was at a seance
(B) it was suddenly recalled by Lou that he was at a seance
(C) Lou suddenly remembered he was at a seance
(D) Lou suddenly found himself remembering he was at a seance
(E) Lou couldn't help but recall that he was at a seance

43. One morning in 1961, the residents of Berlin <u>awoke to find their city divided by</u> a wall.

(A) awoke to find their city divided by
(B) were awakened by the sight of their city being divided by
(C) woke up to see their city divided up by
(D) awoke to find their city will have been divided by
(E) awoke to the sight of the Berlin Wall, dividing the city with

44. A beautiful fountain that cools and entertains visitors in Chicago may actually <u>be controlled through the actions of a remote</u> computer in Denver or Houston.

(A) be controlled through the actions of a remote
(B) be controlled by a
(C) have as its controlling source a
(D) be under the remote control of some
(E) be remotely controlled by the actions of a

45. War may seem exciting in a video game, <u>so the real thing would be</u> terrifying.

(A) so the real thing would be
(B) and the real thing would be
(C) rather the real thing will be
(D) still the real thing is
(E) but the real thing can be

46. Following the success of her anti-slavery novel, *Uncle Tom's Cabin*, Harriet Beecher Stowe published *A Key To Uncle Tom's Cabin* a year <u>later, sequels are not a modern-day phenomenon</u>.

(A) later, sequels are not a modern-day phenomenon
(B) later, therefore sequels are not a modern-day phenomenon
(C) later, proof that sequels are not a modern-day phenomenon
(D) later, sequels not being a modern-day phenomenon
(E) later, one cannot call sequels a modern-day phenomenon

47. More people speak Mandarin <u>as English,</u> French, German, and Japanese combined.

(A) as English,
(B) as much as English,
(C) compared to English,
(D) than speak English,
(E) than the languages of English,

48. Some botanists are worried that trees can feel stressed by changes in the <u>environment; because of this they may stop reproducing</u>.

(A) environment; because of this they may stop reproducing
(B) environment; the result being that they may stop reproducing
(C) environment; then they may stop reproducing
(D) environment, and as a result they may stop reproducing
(E) environment, and may stop reproducing

49. According to several sources, the incidence of diabetes has doubled in the U.S. during the past thirty years.

(A) incidence of diabetes has doubled
(B) incidence of diabetes have doubled
(C) incidents of diabetes have doubled
(D) amount of diabetes has doubled
(E) rate of diabetes have doubled

50. The challenge for any high school history teacher is to make the subject interesting, relevant, and thought-provoking.

(A) to make the subject interesting, relevant, and thought-provoking
(B) to present the subject in a way that is interesting, relevant, and makes the students think
(C) to make students interested, relevant, and thoughtful
(D) to make the subject come alive with interest, relevance, and thoughts
(E) to give the subject interest, relevance, and provocation

51. Action films often begin with ten or fifteen minutes of frantic chase scenes, and it escalates from there, leaving audiences exhausted by the end.

(A) and it escalates from there,
(B) but it escalates from there,
(C) but it escalates from there;
(D) and they escalate from there,
(E) yet they escalate from there,

52. The twentieth century was riddled with the bodies of political leaders who preached non-violence, still they were felled by assassins' bullets.

(A) still they were felled by assassins' bullets
(B) but were felled by assassins' bullets
(C) but were felled by an assassin's bullet
(D) and yet were nevertheless felled by assassins' bullets
(E) but were felled at the hands of an assassin's bullet

53. You can read all the travel books and examine hundreds of photographs, but if you want to know what acres of tulips look like, one has to take a trip to Holland.

(A) one has to take a trip
(B) one must have taken a trip
(C) you have to take a trip
(D) you have to have taken a trip
(E) you got to go

54. According to science, the sun has been burning it's nuclear fuel for billions of years.

(A) has been burning it's
(B) had been burning it's
(C) has been burning its
(D) will have been burning its
(E) is burning it's

Boy, could I use a day off.

Writing Rules! 73

55. Theodore Roosevelt's young <u>wife and his mother both</u> died on the very same day.

(A) wife and his mother both
(B) wife and also his mother both
(C) wife and his mother too
(D) wife and mother also
(E) wife and his mother

56. <u>With global communication being so advanced,</u> it is hard to believe that the world's first artificial satellite, Sputnik 1, was launched into orbit less than sixty years ago.

(A) With global communication being so advanced,
(B) Global communication is now so advanced,
(C) Global communication, having advanced so much,
(D) With all the advancements of global communication,
(E) When one thinks how global communication advanced,

57. Most famous as a prison, the buildings on Alcatraz Island were first built to protect San Francisco's bay area against foreign invasion <u>after they discovered gold</u> there in the late 1840s.

(A) after they discovered gold
(B) after discovering gold was
(C) following gold was discovered
(D) following the discovery of gold
(E) since gold has been discovered

58. The main reason <u>why drivers exhibit road rage is because</u> they have packed their schedules with too many things to do in an impossibly-small amount of time.

(A) why drivers exhibit road rage is because
(B) why drivers exhibit road rage is due to the fact that
(C) drivers exhibit road rage is that
(D) drivers exhibit road rage is because
(E) drivers exhibit road rage can be attributed to the fact that

59. Cult leaders can exert such powerful control <u>over their followers, they</u> may sometimes surrender their will to live.

(A) over their followers, they
(B) that their followers
(C) over their followers, but they
(D) that even their followers
(E) over those following them who

60. Experimenting with dogs in the early 1900s, <u>Ivan Pavlov tried to show</u> that behavior could be modified through a process called conditioning.

(A) Ivan Pavlov tried to show
(B) Ivan Pavlov has shown
(C) it was shown by Ivan Pavlov
(D) they helped Ivan Pavlov show
(E) it had been finally shown by Ivan Pavlov

61. The people in the smaller towns spoke no English, but they were friendly and we communicated as best as we could.

(A) as best as we could
(B) as best as we could have
(C) the best as we could
(D) the best way we could
(E) as well as we could

62. While climbing the tall oak tree to put seeds into the birdhouse, that was when Barry fell sixteen feet straight down and broke both legs.

(A) that was when Barry fell sixteen feet
(B) that was how Barry fell sixteen feet
(C) Barry fell sixteen feet
(D) Barry had fell sixteen feet
(E) Barry wound up falling sixteen feet

63. In 1960, *The Flintstones* became the first animated show on prime-time television, and delaying the bedtime of millions of schoolchildren.

(A) television, and delaying the bedtime of
(B) television, delaying the bedtime of
(C) television, and caused the delayed bedtime of
(D) television; and delayed the bedtime of
(E) television; delaying the bedtime of

64. California has five major league baseball teams, while no other state has more than two.

(A) while no other state has more than two
(B) while no state has more than two
(C) since no other state has more than two
(D) where no other state has more than two
(E) while no other state has had more than two

65. Several audience members grew resentful and even hostile after the speaker seemed to infer that their town was unattractive.

(A) seemed to infer that their
(B) seemed to infer that its
(C) seemingly inferred that their
(D) seemed to imply that their
(E) seemed to suggest that it's

66. If you want to understand the complex language patterns of black crows, your going to need a thick notebook, good listening skills, and a lot of patience.

(A) of black crows, your going to
(B) of black crows, your sure to
(C) for black crows, your going to
(D) of black crows; you're going to
(E) of black crows, you're going to

Writing Rules! 75

67. Stan recalled <u>with some bitterness that</u> he could once fill his car's fuel tank for what it now costs to buy one gallon of gasoline.

(A) with some bitterness that
(B) with any bitterness that
(C) with some bitterness which
(D) through some bitterness that
(E) with barely little bitterness that

68. Africa is home to the world's largest desert, the Sahara, and the fourth-largest <u>island in the world, Madagascar, is there</u>.

(A) island in the world, Madagascar, is there
(B) island in the world, Madagascar, as well
(C) of the world's islands, Madagascar, is there
(D) island, Madagascar
(E) island in the world, which is called Madagascar

69. Jeannette Rankin of Montana, the first woman elected to Congress, was known for <u>her pacifism, besides she supported legislation that</u> protected the rights of women and children.

(A) her pacifism, besides she supported legislation that
(B) her pacifism, plus supporting of legislation that
(C) her pacifism, and her support of legislation that
(D) her pacifism, also supporting legislation which
(E) her pacifism, not to mention she supported legislation that

70. <u>We would reluctantly except an offer of</u> one hundred forty thousand for the house, but we will not let it go for less.

(A) We would reluctantly except an offer of
(B) We would have, with reluctance, except an offer of
(C) It is reluctantly that we would except an offer of
(D) Reluctantly accepting of an offer of
(E) We would reluctantly accept an offer of

71. As with so many artifacts discovered by archeologists at other sites, numerous items found in excavations around Mount Vesuvius <u>that ended up in a museum</u>.

(A) that ended up in a museum
(B) have ended up in a museum
(C) has ended up in a museum
(D) which ended up in a museum
(E) was ending up in a museum

72. The American colonists <u>were comprised of</u> Loyalists who wanted to stay attached to England, revolutionaries who preferred to become independent, and many people who wished the problem would just go away.

(A) were comprised of
(B) were consistent of
(C) contained
(D) comprised
(E) consisted with

Answers to Practice Questions, Part 2

41. **(D)** The word *when* concerns the concept of time, so pairing it with the phrase *the time* is redundant. Answer D completes the sentence clearly, with the fewest words.

    Samantha thought back to the first day of seventh grade, and realized that was when her problems began.

42. **(C)** That entire first section of the sentence (up to the comma) is a participial phrase. The subject -- the person who is laughing -- should appear immediately after the comma. So we can eliminate the first two answer choices. The phrase *suddenly remembered* is short and clear; the corresponding phrases in D and E are longer and clumsy.

    Laughing out loud at the joke his brother had told him earlier, Lou suddenly remembered he was at a seance.

43. **(A)** Two things to watch for. *Residents* is plural, so *their* is needed. Also, make sure *their* is the correct word (not *there* or *they're*). No error.

    One morning in 1961, the residents of Berlin awoke to find their city divided by a wall.

44. **(B)** Again, simpler is almost always better. *By* nicely replaces *through the actions of*, and *remote* isn't needed because the idea of distance is clearly given by the other cities mentioned.

    A beautiful fountain that cools and entertains visitors in Chicago may actually be controlled by a computer in Denver or Houston.

45. **(E)** *Exciting* and *terrifying* in this sentence are intended to show contrast. The conjunction *but* accomplishes this.

    War may seem exciting in a video game, but the real thing can be terrifying.

46. **(C)** As originally written, this is a run-on sentence (technically, a comma splice), and so are answers B and E. Choice D is awkward (it would be a challenge to use the phrase *not being* with any degree of elegance).

    Following the success of her anti-slavery novel, *Uncle Tom's Cabin*, Harriet Beecher Stowe published *A Key To Uncle Tom's Cabin* a year later, proof that sequels are not a modern-day phenomenon.

47. **(D)** The sentence is trying to make a comparison, so the word *More* needs *than* to complete it. Choice D makes the correct comparison between the number of people who speak the languages; choice E does not.

    More people speak Mandarin than speak English, French, German, and Japanese combined.

48. (E) The original sentence uses the vague pronoun *they*, making it unclear whether it's the trees or the botanists that may stop reproducing. Only one of the answers fixes the problem.

Some botanists are worried that trees can feel stressed by changes in the environment, and may stop reproducing.

49. (A) *Incidence* is the correct word, not *incidents*, so it requires the singular verb *has*. Diabetes cases are counted individually, so *amount* is the wrong word (choice D), and *rate* (E) would need the singular *has*. No error.

According to several sources, the incidence of diabetes has doubled in the U.S. during the past thirty years.

50. (A) We're looking for parallel structure here. All three items in the list (*interesting, relevant, thought-provoking*) are adjectives. No error.

The challenge for any high school history teacher is to make the subject interesting, relevant, and thought-provoking.

51. (D) Whether the pronoun *it* refers to *action films* or *chase scenes*, it should be the plural, *they*. The conjunction *but* is the wrong word because there's no twist, surprise, or contradiction in the sentence.

Action films often begin with ten or fifteen minutes of frantic chase scenes, and they escalate from there, leaving audiences exhausted by the end.

52. (B) There were many assassins, so the plural possessive (*assassins'*) is needed. The conjunction *but* helps us avoid the comma splice.

The twentieth century was riddled with the bodies of political leaders who preached non-violence, but were felled by assassins' bullets.

53. (C) Watch for the switch from *you* to *one*, or *one* to *you*.

You can read all the travel books and examine hundreds of photographs, but if you want to know what acres of tulips look like, you have to take a trip to Holland.

54. (C) *It's* is the wrong word. We need the possessive pronoun *its*.

According to science, the sun has been burning its nuclear fuel for billions of years.

55. (E) The sentence ends with the phrase *the same day*, so the word *both* is redundant. Answer E is the simplest and clearest. Also, it might seem as though the word *very* is unnecessary, but it emphasizes the fact that they didn't die just on the same *date*, but on the same *day*, hours apart.

Theodore Roosevelt's young wife and his mother died on the very same day.

56. **(B)** The phrase *being so advanced* is awkward.

Global communication is now so advanced, it is hard to believe...

57. **(D)** The unclear *they* again. The other answers sound terrible; choice E uses the verb *has been*, making the discovery of gold sound recent.

Most famous as a prison, the buildings on Alcatraz Island were first built to protect San Francisco's bay area against foreign invasion following the discovery of gold there in the late 1840s.

58. **(C)** The phrase *reason why* is redundant, doubly so when you add *because*.

The main reason drivers exhibit road rage is that they have packed their schedules with too many things to do in an impossibly-small amount of time.

59. **(B)** Once again, to whom does *they* refer?

Cult leaders can exert such powerful control that their followers may sometimes surrender their will to live.

60. **(A)** *Ivan Pavlov* is the subject and must follow the comma after the participial phrase. So the answer must be either A or B. *Has shown* in choice B is the wrong tense, because it sounds recent. No error.

Experimenting with dogs in the early 1900s, Ivan Pavlov tried to show that behavior could be modified through a process called conditioning.

61. **(E)** Substitute any other superlative for *best* and see how bad it sounds. ("We ran as fastest as we could.") The original sentence could also be changed to end with "the best we could."

The people in the smaller towns spoke no English, but they were friendly and we communicated as well as we could.

62. **(C)** Who was climbing? *Barry* needs to follow the comma. In answer D, *had fell* is never correct. And *wound up falling* is sloppy.

While climbing the tall oak tree to put seeds into the birdhouse, Barry fell sixteen feet straight down and broke both legs.

63. **(B)** If it had said *and delayed*, that would have been fine because *delayed* would match the tense of *became*. Choice D is close, but the semicolon messes things up because it isn't followed by an independent clause (a complete thought). Same with E.

In 1960, *The Flintstones* became the first animated show on prime-time television, delaying the bedtime of millions of schoolchildren.

64. (A) Because California is a state, it can only be compared to other states (the word *other* has to be in there). No error.

California has five major league baseball teams, while no other state has more than two.

65. (D) *Infer* is the wrong word; it means to extract and interpret information from another source. The audience infers something from what the speaker says. The speaker *implies*. Also, *audience* would be singular, but *audience members* is plural.

Several audience members grew resentful and even hostile after the speaker seemed to imply that their town was unattractive.

66. (E) The word is *you're* (you are). The semicolon in D creates a fragment.

If you want to understand the complex language patterns of black crows, you're going to need a thick notebook, good listening skills, and...

67. (A) Read all of the choices in your head. The original is best. No error.

Stan recalled with some bitterness that he could once fill his car's fuel tank...

68. (D) It's the answer that completes the sentence without unnecessary words.

Africa is home to the world's largest desert, the Sahara, and the fourth-largest island, Madagascar.

69. (C) The phrase *her pacifism* creates the need for a similar phrase to provide parallel structure. We also need a conjunction, such as *and*, after the comma. The word *besides* creates a comma splice, or run-on sentence.

...was known for her pacifism, and her support of legislation that...

70. (E) *Except* is the wrong word. We need *accept*.

We would reluctantly accept an offer...

71. (B) The original sentence is two dependent clauses. There's a verb missing.

As with so many artifacts discovered by archeologists at other sites, numerous items found in excavations around Mount Vesuvius have ended up in a museum.

72. (D) *Composed of* or *consisted of* -- okay. *Comprised of* -- no good.

The American colonists comprised Loyalists who wanted to stay attached to England, revolutionaries who preferred to become independent, and many people who wished the problem would just go away.

Practice Questions
Part 3: Paragraphs

This section presents an early draft of a short essay. The writing is understandable, but it needs work. Some of the questions will ask you to correct errors in individual sentences. Others will ask you to improve the structure of a paragraph, by rearranging or combining sentences, for example. And still others will ask you to consider the sentence or paragraph that would best complete the given essay, and select it from among the five answer choices.

Based on everything we've already covered, most of this is easy. What's new is the task of reorganizing. When you're dealing with paragraphs, you have to hold one or two (or three) sentences in your head at once, and be able to mentally juggle them around. (As with so much of this stuff, it helps to read silently, but in a voice that you can hear in your mind.)

On most standardized tests featuring a writing and grammar section, this type of question usually represents a small portion of the exam. The SAT, for example, will have just six of these questions, based on one writing sample. We'll work on two essays, with six questions based on each. It'll be a good final step before we get into writing entire essays ourselves. But before we get started, here's a short checklist of things to watch for. If you're pretty sure you understand what each item is about -- and are confident you can find and correct related errors -- check its box and move on. If not, go back to earlier pages in this book and review. (Don't you hate to hear the word *review*? It's like when you get finished painting a room and somebody comes in and tells you it needs another coat. Not what you want to hear. But with just a little more effort, the results will be much better. You'll see.)

↓	
10	☐ Apostrophes & contractions
27	☐ Comparatives & superlatives
28	☐ Redundancy
35	☐ Sentence fragments
35	☐ Run-on sentences & comma splices
39	☐ Subject and object pronouns
39	☐ Prepositions
41	☐ Participial phrases and subjects
43	☐ Subject-verb agreement
46	☐ Verb tense errors
50	☐ Parallel structure
52	☐ Misplaced modifiers
54	☐ Semicolons
55	☐ Conjunctions
56	☐ Adverbs
58	☐ Vague pronouns

Writing Rules!

Questions 73-78 are based on the passage below.
Notice that each sentence in the passage is numbered.
Correct answers and their explanations are on pages 84 and 85.

(1) One of the great ironies of an increased threat of global terrorism is that it causes people to travel less, interact with other cultures less, and grow more fearful and suspicious of faraway places and their inhabitants. (2) If the solution to terrorism is greater understanding among nations, the problem itself becomes a self-perpetuating process.

(3) As citizens and governments close themselves in and isolate themselves, they grow less familiar with those who are different. (4) They cling ever more rigid to what they have grown up with, their own ways of life, beliefs, and practices. (5) Soon, the differences grow into mutual suspicion, perceived slights, and the root cause of any negative issues that may arise among nations. (6) *Foreign* becomes synonymous with *evil*. (7) International relations, then, turn into dry woodlands in the middle of a hot summer's drought. (8) Under such conditions, any source of combustion, even a small spark, can be enough to start a blaze that quickly grows out of control, damaging everything in its path.

(9) Verbal threats and overtly hostile acts originating from either side are met by the other with shock, confusion, and people expressing their outrage. (10) More threats are exchanged, followed by more violence. (11) Than another round of shock, confusion, and outrage. (12) As the fire turns to an all-out conflagration, those who suffer most are the innocent bystanders: men, women, and children who are just trying to live their lives, and who have the least control over the circumstances that led to the hostility in the first place.

(13) After some length of time, a point of desperation is usually reached. (14) Then, one side reaches out a hand to the other. (15) It may be a gesture of friendship. (16) More likely, it's the result of fear, fatigue, financial burden, and growing dissent at home. (17) The first step to peace is acknowledged to be communication and at least some attempt at understanding. (18) If only they had tried that at the beginning, maybe the flood of death and destruction could have been avoided.

73. Which of the following revisions would improve sentence 3?

(A) Change *those* to *them*
(B) Change *close* to *are closing*
(C) Delete *close themselves in and*
(D) Insert *and* before *they*
(E) Delete *less*

74. Which of the following would be the best version of sentence 4?

(A) They are clinging ever more rigid to what they had grown up with, their own beliefs and practices.
(B) As they cling ever more rigidly to what they had grown up with; their ways of life and beliefs.
(C) However, they cling more rigidly to what they grew up with, their own ways of life, beliefs, and practices.
(D) They cling ever more rigidly to what they have grown up with, their own ways of life, beliefs, and practices.
(E) (Keep it as it is.)

75. Which improves sentence 9?

(A) Delete *overtly*
(B) Delete *people expressing their*
(C) Replace *their* with *they're*
(D) Begin the sentence with *Next,*
(E) Delete the comma after *confusion*

76. Which corrects sentence 11?

(A) Replace *than* with *then*
(B) Delete *round of*
(C) Replace *another* with *other*
(D) Change *outrage* to *outraged*
(E) Delete all commas

77. Which of the following would be the best revision that combines sentences 13 and 14?

(A) Some time having gone by, a desperation point is reached, usually, and one side reaches out a hand to the other.
(B) Usually, after some length of time, a point of desperation having been reached, one side offers the other a hand.
(C) After waiting some amount of time and then feeling desperate, one side usually reaches out a hand to the other side.
(D) With a point of desperation usually reached after some length of time, one side reaches out a hand to the other.
(E) After some length of time, usually at the point of desperation, one side reaches out a hand to the other.

78. How could the underlined part of sentence 18 be changed to keep it consistent with an earlier metaphor for terrorism?

If only they had tried that at the beginning, <u>maybe the flood of death and destruction could have been avoided</u>.

(A) maybe the fire could have been extinguished before it had a chance to spread.
(B) the feuding might have ended.
(C) peace may have come sooner.
(D) the trees may have been able to find water.
(E) there would be no need for shock and outrage.

Writing Rules! 83

Answers and Explanations
Questions 73-78

73. **(C)** The two phrases, *close themselves in* and *isolate themselves*, are redundant; neither adds any new information not provided by the other. Answer C is the only choice that allows you to eliminate one of them.

The other answers all create problems that aren't there in the original sentence. For example, answer D inserts the conjunction *and* between the two clauses, as though they were both complete thoughts. But the first clause begins with *as*, making it dependent. Answer E changes the meaning of the sentence and contradicts the entire essay.

Here's the revision:

> As citizens and governments isolate themselves, they grow less familiar with those who are different.

74. **(D)** Sentence 4 has only one problem: the word *rigid* is intended to modify the verb *cling*, so it needs to be an adverb. Change *rigid* to *rigidly* and you're done. Answers A and E don't make the necessary change. Answer B puts a semicolon after a dependent clause, and you already know that a semicolon is used to separate two complete thoughts. And choice C uses the word *However*, which we would expect to introduce an idea that is somehow opposite to the one expressed in sentence 3. But sentence 4 elaborates on sentence 3, so the *However* doesn't make sense.

> They cling ever more rigidly to what they have grown up with, their own ways of life, beliefs, and practices.

75. **(B)** Sentence 9 includes a list of three items; all of these items should be in the same form. Answer B allows us to remove the long and unnecessary phrase *people expressing their*, leaving three one-word nouns.

The other answer choices make little or no sense. The word *overtly* is not an error. Choice C looks to replace the correct word *their* with the incorrect *they're*. And answer D's *Next* suggests that there's a sequence of events being continued; in fact, sentences 7 and 8 introduce an abstract idea (foreign relations as dried forest), and sentence 9 provides a concrete example based on that abstraction.

> Verbal threats and overtly hostile acts originating from either side are met by the other with shock, confusion, and outrage.

76. (A) *Than* is the wrong word; it's used for comparisons. The correct word is *then*, used to indicate a sequence in time.

You may have noticed that sentence 11 isn't even a sentence. This is an example of using a fragment appropriately; the writer is trying to convey a fast pace, a sense that things are happening one after another and escalating. However, if one of the questions had addressed this, changing the fragment into a grammatically-correct complete sentence, that complete sentence would probably be the answer you should choose.

> Then another round of shock, confusion, and outrage.

77. (E) Look at the phrases that have been created for answers A, B, C, and D:

- *Some time having gone by*
- *a point of desperation having been reached*
- *waiting some amount of time and then feeling desperate*
- *with a point of desperation usually reached*

Is there a good reason to resort to such awkward langauge? No, because answer E does the job, more clearly and with fewer words:

> After some length of time, usually at the point of desperation, one side reaches out a hand to the other.

78. (A) The metaphor in sentences 7 and 8 was that of a dry forest in danger of bursting into flames; this imagery was used to represent the state of international relations when countries become suspicious of each other.

In sentence 18, the metaphor changes to that of a flood. Same idea, but not consistent. The only answer choice that returns to the out-of-control fire metaphor is E:

> If only they had tried that at the beginning, maybe the fire could have been extinguished before it had a chance to spread.

Questions 79-84 are based on the passage below.
Notice that each sentence in the passage is numbered.
Correct answers and their explanations are on pages 88 and 89.

(1) I'd like to mainly tell you about something weird that happened last year. (2) My friend Jack and me are walking along the street in front of my house, and a police car pulled up. (3) There were two officers inside, both were eating cheeseburgers and drinking root beer.

(4) The officers asked if we'd seen a rottweiler, wearing a plaid jacket and red bowtie, riding a blue unicycle. (5) Of course we had to stop and think for a minute, just to make sure, but we said, no, we hadn't seen him. (6) Then Jack, who likes to be a wiseguy, said, "Wait, did you say a red bowtie and blue unicycle, or a blue bowtie and red unicycle?" (7) Like we had been seeing rottweilers riding unicycles all day, and he wanted to be sure he knew which one they meant. (8) I don't think the officers appreciated Jack's humor, because they drove away without answering.

(9) Now guess how much time went by? (10) It was no more than ten minutes later, and out of the woods rode a dog on a unicycle wearing a plaid jacket and a red bowtie. (11) He was coming straight at us, and I noticed he was also

juggling five snowballs! (12) He stopped next to us and he said, "Man, if you guys had a video camera right now, you could make a lot of money with this." (13) Then he turned around and rode back into the woods, and we never saw him again. (14) Now here's the weird part: it was July. (15) So, I mean, where did he get the snowballs?

79. Which of the following revisions would improve sentence 1?

(A) Change *happened* to *happens*
(B) Change *mainly* to *mostly*
(C) Delete *mainly*
(D) Insert *all* between *you* and *about*
(E) Change *something weird* to *a weird thing*

80. Which of the following would be the best version of sentence 2?

(A) My friend Jack and me was walking along the street in front of my house, and a police car pulled up.
(B) My friend Jack and me were walking along the street in front of my house, and a police car pulled up.
(C) My friend Jack and I were walking along the street in front of my house when a police car pulled up.
(D) As my friend Jack and I were walking along the street in front of my house, and a police car pulled up.
(E) (Keep it as it is.)

81. Which of the following would be the best version of sentence 3?

(A) There were two officers inside, both eating cheeseburgers and drinking root beer.
(B) There were two officers inside; both eating cheeseburgers and drinking root beer.
(C) The two officers inside both eating cheeseburgers and drinking root beer.
(D) There were two officers inside, and they were both eating cheeseburgers and drinking root beer at the same time.
(E) Two officers, who could be seen eating cheeseburgers and drinking root beer, were inside.

82. Which of the following revisions would improve the underlined portion of sentence 7 (below)?

<u>Like we had been seeing rottweilers riding unicycles all day,</u> and he wanted to be sure he knew which one they meant.

(A) (Keep it as it is.)
(B) Like we had seen rottweilers riding unicycles all day,
(C) He asked it like we saw rottweilers riding unicycles all day,
(D) He asked this as though we had been seeing rottweilers on unicycles all day,
(E) As if rottweilers riding unicycles all day was what we saw,

83. What would correct the punctuation problem in sentence 9?

(A) Insert a comma after *guess*
(B) Change the question mark to a period
(C) Insert a comma after *Now*
(D) Insert a semicolon after *guess*
(E) Put quotation marks around *by*

84. What would improve sentence 15?

(A) Change *So* to *Like*
(B) Change *did* to *does*
(C) Change *the* to *those*
(D) Replace *where* with *how*
(E) Delete *I mean* and both commas

Answers and Explanations
Questions 79-84

79. (C) The word *mainly* doesn't have a purpose in this sentence. Take it out and read the sentence, and you'll see that there's no loss of meaning. Changing to the present tense, *happens* (answer A), is wrong because the incident is in the past. The word *mostly* would be just as meaningless as *mainly*, so answer B is out. In answer D, the word *all* would be confusing: is the writer trying to say *you all* or *all about*? And choice E presents another useless change -- nothing is accomplished by replacing *something weird* to *a weird thing*.

   I'd like to tell you about something weird that happened last year.

80. (C) Because the subject consists of the two people walking along the street, the subject pronoun *I* is needed. Also, the story involves an incident that happened last year. The present tense could be used, but a quick check of the rest of the passage shows that the other verbs are all in the past tense. So the verb in sentence 2 should be *were* walking.

   The only possible choices, then are C and D. Answer D, though, is not a complete sentence; it contains two dependent clauses. The answer has to be C.

   My friend Jack and I were walking along the street
   in front of my house when a police car pulled up.

81. (A) As originally written, the sentence is really two complete thoughts separated by a comma; that's a comma splice, a first cousin of the run-on sentence. It has to be fixed.

   Answer B inserts a semicolon, but notice that the verb *were* has been removed. Now the second half of the sentence is a dependent clause and, therefore, a sentence fragment. So the semicolon doesn't work.

   Answer C is another fragment (again, the verb *were* is missing).

   Answer D adds the phrase *at the same time*, which is redundant (if they were both eating, obviously it was at the same time).

   Answer E rearranges the phrases needlessly. *Could be seen* by whom?

   As usual, the best answer is the one that provides the simplest, clearest sentence, free of grammar and punctuation errors:

   There were two officers inside, both eating
   cheeseburgers and drinking root beer.

Writing Rules!

82. (D) The sentence may be funnier the way it's written, but the use of the word *Like* in this context is incorrect. *Like* should be used to compare things. For example: "That cat looks like a flying squirrel." As opposed to: "That cat looks as though he's flying." (See page 27 for more about this rule.)

Also, the original isn't even a complete sentence; as long as it is, it's still a fragment. So answers A and B are unacceptable, because they don't correct the fragment problem. Answer C does, but it keeps the use of *like*, so we have to reject it, as well. Answer E introduces the clumsy phrase *was what we saw*, and takes us back to a fragment. Only D fixes the two mistakes, and does so without unnecessary words.

He asked this as though we had been seeing rottweilers on unicycles all day,

83. (B) You need a question mark when asking something, such as, "How much time went by?" But you don't need one when telling someone to guess how much time went by. That's a command, not a question. (This seems picky, I know. See page 33 for more examples.) Answer D could work if it had said to insert a colon after *guess:* "Now guess: how much time went by?" But that seems strange in the context. The best solution, really, would be to delete sentence 9. However, the question asks for correction, not removal, so we're left with answer B.

Now guess how much time went by.

84. (E) All of the other answers either fail to correct anything (C and D) or create an error that wasn't there before (A and B). The problem with the phrase *I mean* is that it's sloppy, too informal, and meaningless in this context.

So where did he get the snowballs?

Writing Rules! 89

Questions 85-90 are based on the passage below.
Correct answers and their explanations are on pages 92 and 93.

(1) When studying history, the information grows more abundant and more detailed as we get closer to the present. **(2)** This should not seem surprising, because over the years there have been such dramatic advances in the documentation, transmission, and preservation of historical records. **(3)** An event that took place thousands of years ago may have been written about by a single witness; if we're lucky. **(4)** Just as likely, that history was passed down orally from person to person, over many generations.

(5) The first historian to record some version of the account in writing may not have been born when the event took place. **(6)** Also, the emphasis we now place on names and dates may not be what someone writing back then may have thought was important.

(7) But often, that person's account is all we have. **(8)** When we talk about the ancient Greeks, for example, we aren't sure what century Homer lived in, or if he even existed.

(9) We know a lot about Galileo and Napoleon Bonaparte, but still there are gaps. **(10)** Our understanding of Abraham Lincoln and Susan B. Anthony are rich and voluminous, because we can read what they wrote, as well as what others wrote about them. **(11)** In the case of John F. Kennedy, there are more books about his assassination than about most other presidents' *entire lives*.

(12) If our knowledge of the distant past is skimpy, we in the present have a very different kind of dilemma. **(13)** Access to far more details about people than we ever needed or wanted.

85. Which of the following would be the best version of sentence 1?

(A) When studying history, we find that the information grows more abundant and more detailed as we get closer to the present.
(B) When studying history, it's clear that the information grows more abundant and more detailed as we get closer to the present.
(C) The more we study history, the information grows more abundant and more detailed as we get closer to the present.
(D) As we continue to study history, the more abundantly and detailed the information grows as we get closer to the present.
(E) While history is being studied, the information grows more abundant and more detailed as we get closer to the present.

86. Which of the following revisions would improve sentence 3?

(A) Change *if* to *and yet*
(B) Change *written* to *wrote*
(C) Make the semicolon a comma
(D) Change *took* to *had taken*
(E) (Keep it as it is.)

87. Which improves sentence 6?

(A) (Keep it as it is.)
(B) Change *what* to *which*
(C) Replace *the emphasis we now place* with *our emphasis*
(D) Change *may have thought* to *would have thought*
(E) Change *was important* to *had importance*.

88. Which of the following would work well as a transition between sentences 8 and 9?

(A) That's why historians tend to ignore the issue.
(B) Still, he is revered for his best works, *The Iliad* and *The Odyssey*.
(C) We have some information about people living in Central America about 10,000 years ago.
(D) After the invention of the printing press in the 1400s, the situation steadily improved.
(E) Things are much better now.

89. Which of the following revisions would improve the underlined portion of sentence 10 (below)?

Our understanding of Abraham Lincoln and Susan B. Anthony <u>are rich and voluminous, because we can</u> read what they wrote, as well as what others wrote about them.

(A) fill volumes, because we can
(B) are complete and numerous, since we are able to
(C) are rich and voluminous, we can
(D) is rich and voluminous; however, we can
(E) is rich and voluminous, because we can

90. What is the best way to combine sentences 12 and 13?

(A) Insert *and* after *dilemma*
(B) Insert a colon after *dilemma*
(C) Insert a semicolon after *dilemma*
(D) Delete the first period and *That is*
(E) Make the first period a comma

Answers and Explanations
Questions 85-90

85. (A) The problem with the original sentence is that it begins with a phrase that is supposed to modify the subject. Who is studying history? The information isn't studying; it's part of what's being studied. In this sentence, we are studying history, so the subject (*we*) must follow that opening clause.

Answer B continues the problem. Choices D and E are just clumsy rearrangements -- D uses *as* in two different clauses, while E uses *while* and *as*. Both are a little confusing. Answer C could be made to work, but we'd have to go out of our way to avoid using the word *more* four times. Answer A is fine.

> When studying history, we find that the information grows more abundant and more detailed as we get closer to the present.

86. (C) The clauses on both sides of the semicolon have to be complete sentences on their own. In this case, *if we're lucky* is a fragment. The easiest way to fix it is to simply change the semicolon to a comma.

Answer A still doesn't turn the fragment into an independent clause. Answer B sounds terrible (*may have been wrote*), while D tries to use two very different verb tenses for the same event. Choice E is no help. Only C works.

> An event that took place thousands of years ago may have been written about by a single witness, if we're lucky.

87. (D) The phrases *may not be* and *may have thought* are competing with each other. Changing the second one to *would have thought* just sounds better. The uncertainty of the statement is maintained by the remaining phrase *may not be*.

Answer A solves nothing, and B is worse. Answer C isn't a bad idea -- it tries to use fewer words to say the same thing -- but the *may* and *may* problem is still there. Choice E is a sidestep, and doesn't really change the sentence at all. Plug in D and read it out loud. Isn't that better?

> Also, the emphasis we now place on names and dates may not be what someone writing back then would have thought was important.

88. (D) The passage is saying that the information we have about events that took place thousands of years ago is sketchy and sometimes unreliable, but that as we approach the present, our knowledge grows in quantity and detail.

Homer and the ancient Greeks are used as an example from a long time ago (8th century BCE). If we look ahead a little in the passage, we can see that Galileo and Napoleon are mentioned, followed by Lincoln, Anthony, and Kennedy. So there's a chronological sequence: Galileo was born in 1564, Napoleon in 1769, Lincoln in 1809, Anthony in 1820, and Kennedy in 1917.

The question asks for a transition between sentences 8 and 9. Sentence 8 talks about Homer and sentence 9 refers to Galileo and Napoleon. In this span of two sentences, then, we go from knowing very little about Homer to knowing quite a bit about Galileo and Napoleon. Which of the answer choices would be a good bridge between the two?

Answer A addresses only the issues of Homer's time and existence, so it doesn't help at all. Answer B, also, sticks with Homer and his writings. Choice C goes the wrong way, back to 10,000 years ago. Answer E takes us immediately to the present, which is not a transition to Galileo. But look at choice D. It brings in the invention of the printing press in the 1400s, and offers a possible explanation for the subsequent increase in our historical knowledge. That has to be the one.

> After the invention of the printing press in the 1400s, the situation steadily improved.

89. (E) This is a matter of subject-verb agreement. The subject is *understanding*, which is singular, so the verb has to be singular (*is*). We are thrown off, possibly, by the fact that Lincoln and Anthony are two people. But the sentence isn't talking about them; rather, it's talking about our understanding of them.

Two answers give us the singular verb we need: D and E. Answer D's use of the word *however* doesn't make sense, though, because it makes it sound as if the second part of the sentence is going to contrast or contradict the first (which it doesn't). That leaves us with E:

> Our understanding of Abraham Lincoln and Susan B. Anthony is rich and voluminous, because we can read what they wrote, as well as what others wrote about them.

90. (B) Sentence 12 sets us up for a revelation of some kind, but then doesn't deliver. Instead, it waits for sentence 13 to show up with the payoff. Sentence 13 has its own problems; it's a fragment, and needs to be fixed. The best solution is a colon after *dilemma*, neatly combining the two sentences. The colon is like an arrow: pointing to the next idea (see how that worked right there?) Watch again:

> If our knowledge of the distant past is skimpy, we in the present have a very different kind of dilemma: access to far more details about people than we ever needed or wanted.

Essays

No more multiple choice questions, so no more chances to guess. Now you have to actually write something. In any context, there are certain things you should always do, certain things you should never do, and certain things you could do, depending on the situation. Let's start with the Number One Rule, the thing you should always do, whether you're taking a math test, doing your science homework, writing a college application essay, reciting your wedding vows, or talking to the judge in small claims court:

Answer the question!

Follow instructions. Do the assignment. You can give the best response in the history of the world, but if you're answering the wrong question, there's going to be trouble. For example, let's say you're writing an essay on a standardized test, such as the SAT. The assignment is to consider the value and legitimacy of scientific studies that analyze the possible health risks associated with certain foods or drugs. Too boring? Okay, try this. The assignment is to discuss dangerous activities (climbing the Matterhorn, bungee jumping from the Eiffel Tower, storming the ring at Wrestlemania). The actual question: "Is it better to lead a long, safe, and uneventful life, or take risks and seek thrills, knowing you could be killed at a young age? Assess both sides of the argument, then choose one, supporting it with examples from your education, extracurricular reading, and personal experience."

The clock is ticking, and you barely stop to think before starting to write. You remember that your grandfather -- the one you never met -- lost his life in a stampede while hunting blue wildebeest in Botswana. You know very little about hunting, aren't sure if blue wildebeest are really blue, and have no idea where Botswana is. But it's a real-life experience, so off you go.

It's a perfect topic, right on target; your grandfather was a risk-taker, a thrill-seeker, and died young because of it! Unfortunately, you run yourself off the track and focus on the evils of hunting and the poor, endangered wildebeest who shouldn't be shot, but should be allowed to wander into crocodile-infested rivers to be chewed alive just like they do on TV.

The assignment, of course, was to discuss the conscious decision to jeopardize your own life by participating in dangerous activities, and to weigh the resulting thrills against a long (and presumably dull) life. Again, it doesn't matter how brilliant your essay is. Fail to answer the question and you're going to get a low score -- possibly even a zero.

If you're working on a homework assignment or a college essay, give yourself a chance to think before you start writing. Even if time is limited (the Essay section of the SAT, for example, is just 25 minutes), focus on the topic and try to mentally plan the path you're going to follow; then stay on the path. Remember where you want to end up and keep moving in that direction.

Who's the reader?

The second thing to consider is your audience. If you're doing a book report that you're going to present to the class, and you're the only one who's read the book, you'll need to explain the general plot and the main characters. If it's a book the whole class has read, and the assignment is to concentrate on some specific aspect of the story, then you can dive right in.

So who is the reader? If it's your teacher, you're probably trying to demonstrate what you've learned and what you think. But it's also possible that you're writing about a subject with which your teacher is unfamiliar (your recent family reunion on Easter Island, for example), and in that case you'd be the expert, teaching the teacher. When working on an essay for a standardized test, always make sure that after wandering off to some exotic example, metaphor, or anecdote, *you can find your way back to the assigned topic*. You'll also want to be as careful as possible about spelling and grammar. Sending an email to your stupid cousin Freddie? Relax and just say what you want to say. (Freddie wouldn't know a possessive pronoun from a parking meter anyway.)

Start at the beginning!

Have you ever missed the first fifteen minutes of a movie and spent the rest of the time trying to figure out what was going on? It's frustrating. Don't forget: you have all of that background information in your mind that helps you make sense of what you're saying. But your readers don't; all they have is what you tell them. So try to picture the person you're talking to as you write. And don't change that person anywhere along the way. Keeping the intended audience clearly in mind will help you maintain your voice, and your tone.

My what?

You know exactly what I'm talking about. You've heard it before: Lower your voice, mister. You'd better change that tone, young lady. Well, that's not exactly it. The voice in a written work is a combination of point of view and level of authority. Who's talking? If you were to read a pamphlet from the Department of Justice and a poem by Emily Dickinson, they would have different voices. Don't believe me? Hear, listen for yourself:

US Department of Justice, Mission Statement

> "...to enforce the law and defend the interests of the United States according to the law; to ensure public safety against threats foreign and domestic; to provide federal leadership in preventing and controlling crime; to seek just punishment for those guilty of unlawful behavior; and to ensure fair and impartial administration of justice for all Americans."

Emily Dickinson, untitled poem

> " If I can stop one heart from breaking,
> I shall not live in vain;
> If I can ease one life the aching,
> Or cool one pain,
> Or help one fainting robin
> Unto his nest again,
> I shall not live in vain."

Both excerpts have something to do with helping others, but the voices couldn't be more different. Can you even imagine Emily Dickinson writing those words from the DOJ mission statement? Or the Department of Justice ever publishing anything resembling Dickinson's poem?

Voice also includes point of view. Are you an all-knowing narrator? Someone involved in the content? An outside observer? And how are you addressing your audience? Are you speaking directly to the reader, or just speaking? These elements are all part of voice. But so is the language you use, your choice of words, sentence structure, and even punctuation. Voice is a combination of what you say and how you say it.

Okay, so what's tone? It's more about feeling: how the author feels about the subject, and how the reader feels after reading what the author has written. If you're reading a letter from someone who's angry, you can usually sense the emotion in the words; that's the author's tone coming through. Or maybe the tone is sarcastic, depressed, funny, condescending, or any number of other feelings. (I'm thinking now that there's no need to spend too much time on voice and tone, because the more you talk about something like this, the more confusing it seems to get.) Let's just say that a writer usually writes in one voice, but that one voice can have many different tones. If you're in school, your teachers probably all have teachers' voices, but it's very likely that their tones are not the same: one may be cold and distant, another may be warm and chummy, a third may be nervous and unsure.

That's enough about that. Let's pretend that we're writing an essay together. We'll start with the assigned topic and see what happens. (Remember: the assignment is what's *under* the box, not what's inside of it.) If any new rules pop up that we haven't already discussed, we'll talk about them as we go.

Does that sound like fun? I know, but let's do it anyway.

Essay 1

"The function of wisdom is to discriminate between good and evil." -- Cicero

Assignment:
Is evil necessary in order for good to exist? Choose a position on this question, then compose an essay supporting your point of view. Be sure to use sound reasoning. You may also draw on examples from your studies, observations, and personal experiences.

    This is a big question. The issue of good and evil is one that philosophers have been wrestling with for thousands of years. And they still haven't figured it out, so I guess that means philosophers aren't good wrestlers. (Already my mind is wandering. I'm picturing Socrates in tights, being pinned by Achilles, while Hercules hits Plato over the head with a folding chair. The referee, Aristotle, is distracted by the puzzle of whether or not the entire arena really exists.) (This is bad. I just lost forty seconds and haven't written a word yet. Have to focus.)

    Okay. Good and evil. I guess I have two choices: Either good can exist without evil, or it can't. What do I think? I have to try to step out of my little world and see Good and Evil on some kind of grand scale.

    I don't see how good can exist without its opposite, because there would be no way to make a comparison. If there were only good people and someone came up to you and said, "Wow, you're really a good person," you would be confused. It would have the same effect as if they said, "Wow, you

were born." A fish doesn't know it's in the water until you take him out. When he can see the difference, then he understands water, but until then, he doesn't know what you're talking about. It's as though you'd just said to him, "Wow, you were hatched." (I'm ignoring the fact that fish have little aptitude for abstract conversation and almost never know what you're talking about.)

    What examples or experiences can I come up with? I'm really trying to resist using Hitler as an example of evil, because I bet every person writing this essay is making some reference to him. His name has become a synonym for evil, so it's too easy, too much of a cliche -- true, but boring. What else can I use to illustrate evil? I like the fish thing, and I'm definitely going to work that in. It's just that I need to talk about evil in a concrete way.

Writing Rules!

I'm thinking about this as two different questions: "Can good exist if there has never been any evil?" and "Can good exist if there was evil, but we got rid of it?" I think it's something like the difference between someone who is blind from birth (she could never see) and someone who lost her vision later in life (she can't see but remembers what it was like). If I break it into two separate questions, the person reading my essay will be taken by surprise, and will be impressed by the amount of thought I've put into this. I hope.

It seems pretty obvious that everyone doing this assignment is going to come to the same conclusion: we can't appreciate Good if we have no understanding of Evil. The concept of Good is a comparison. If I say, "This soup is good," I must be rating it according to some standard or scale. There has to be the possibility that soup could be bad, or it's meaningless to say it's good. Or if I say the soup is hot, it's understood that the temperature of the soup *could be* lower. Temperature is a good analogy, I think, because it's a scale. The scale has extremes, and you can go from one extreme to the other by taking small steps in a certain direction.

Okay, how should I start this thing? I think I'll mention the philosophers. That strikes a nice tone, as though I've been spending a good deal of my spare time reading philosophy.

> **Good without Evil?**
> Philosophers have ~~always~~ been struggling with the ~~question~~ meaning of Good and Evil since the beginning of time, or at least since people started thinking. It seems clear, then, that Evil has always been around. The question is, does ~~it have to?~~

I like this, because I've restated the question in my own words.

Evil have to exist?

Then I'll divide the question into the two parts I came up with:

> Maybe this is really two ~~separate~~ questions. The first ~~question~~ is, could we ever have learned to recognize Good if Evil never existed? The second ~~question~~ is, if we could somehow get rid of Evil (but (hold onto) our collective memory of it~~s existence~~), could we (keep identifying) and appreciate the concept of Good?

retain

continue to identify

Should I state my opinion right up front, then try to defend it? Or should I write the essay as if I'm figuring it out as I go along, and come to a conclusion at the end? I'm not sure. Let's see what happens when I develop the two questions I've raised. I think I'll use the temperature thing next.

> Addressing the first question, ~~it seems to me~~ that without Evil, Good would be meaningless. Imagine an island where the temperature is always exactly seventy-six degrees, day and night. The island has been inhabited for thousands of years by people with absolutely no contact with the rest of the world, and they know nothing of weather patterns and temperature fluctuations. In fact, they don't even have a *word* for temperature, because no one on the island has ever talked about it. They are an entire population of short-sleeved, croquet-playing, backyard gardeners who have never seen a coat or a pair of mittens. One day, a man from northern Finland makes an emergency landing of his single-engine plane on the island. After getting out of his ~~plane~~, the man looks at the shocked faces staring back at him and says, "My, it certainly is warm here!" (He says this in Finnish, but that doesn't matter, because they won't know what he means anyway, even if he were speaking their language.) The point is, it feels warm to him, because he knows what cold feels like. They don't feel warm, because they've never felt cold.

(Margin notes: "I think" replacing "it seems to me"; "aircraft" replacing "plane"; "Separate sentences: the world. They...")

I like that idea about the fish being unaware of water. I think it would fit in well right here, because it's less complicated and easier to understand than the island analogy. Actually, maybe it should come first?

> Another example: A fish living its entire life in the depths of the ocean has no idea that it's in water. It perceives other fish -- predator and prey -- as well as plants and rocks. But it has never experienced dry land or even air, so it has no such concept, ~~and without it, there's no need for the idea of water.~~ Now take that fish out of the ocean and wave it around in the ~~air~~, and it suddenly understands that there's a water place and a no-water place; the fish begins to develop a preference.

(Margin notes: "and therefore has no need for the concept of water."; "put this before island story"; "breeze")

Now I come to a conclusion about the first question:

> The idea of Good without Evil reminds me of the island where the temperature never changes, or the fish that has never been out of the ocean. Without contrast, without something that's different, there's no way to identify a ~~description of something~~ condition. ~~You need something to measure against.~~

(Margin note: "switch")

Writing Rules!

What about the second question? What would happen if Evil did exist, but somehow we could get rid of it? Would we be able to stay Good forever, and would we know? I think we have to jump into the distant future, because I can't picture a world without evil anytime soon.

> Now let's imagine some time in the future when ~~all~~ Evil has been ~~totally~~ eliminated, but people still have some understanding of the concept. Books and movies exist showing what we were like in the early years of the twenty-first century. The front pages of daily newspapers from our time are laminated and mounted on classroom walls, so schoolchildren can learn about the horrors of the past. ~~Entire museums are dedicated to Evil, and families visit them while on vacation.~~ There are even Evil deniers, who claim it's all a hoax and that such a thing ~~wasn't real~~ could never have existed.

Families on vacation visit museums that are devoted entirely to Evil.

conspiracy theorists

That seems silly, like some bad science fiction story. No matter how far we go into the future, we're still talking about human beings. I doubt that our basic nature is going to change much. Purely good behavior is not possible.

insert: Is that really how it would be?

> More likely, if we could get rid of Evil, the Good that remained would be divided into different grades of good. Eventually, the bottom of the scale would be considered Evil ("What? You only did fifty-two hours of volunteer work last week? What kind of monster are you?"), and we'd be right back where we started. Except without the wars and the murders and the child abuse.

Conclusion:

out

combine: same thing, each necessary for the...

> No, I don't think Good can exist with Evil. They are ~~just~~ two sides of the same thing. Each is necessary for the other's existence. But here's an ~~interesting~~ experiment we could try:
>
> We start with a group of some social mammal, maybe prairie dogs. They seem to have developed a complex system of cooperation in which they keep each other out of danger by warning the group when a predator is approaching. If we think of the predator as Evil and the prairie dog group as Good, what would happen if we removed the ~~Evil~~ predators completely? Isolate the prairie dogs inside some kind of protective bubble, where they have food, water, and air -- but no threat. Would they live happily ever after? Or would they eventually turn on each other? Would we see Evil return?

springing from within Good itself?

Good without Evil?

Philosophers have been struggling with the meaning of good and evil since the beginning of time, or at least since people started thinking. It seems clear, then, that evil has always been around. The question is, does Evil have to exist?

Maybe this is really two questions. Could we ever have learned to recognize Good if Evil never existed? And if we could somehow get rid of Evil (but retain our collective memory of it), could we continue to identify and appreciate the concept of Good?

Addressing the first question, I think that without Evil, Good would be meaningless. A fish living its entire life in the depths of the ocean has no idea that it's in water. It perceives other fish -- predator and prey -- as well as plants and rocks. But the fish has never experienced dry land or even air, so it has no such concept, and therefore has no need for the concept of water. Now take that fish out of the ocean and wave it around in the breeze, and it suddenly understands that there's a water place and a no-water place; the fish begins to develop a preference.

Another example: Imagine an island where the temperature is always exactly seventy-six degrees, day and night. The island has been inhabited for thousands of years by people with absolutely no contact with the rest of the world. They know nothing of weather patterns and temperature fluctuations. In fact, they don't even have a *word* for temperature, because no one on the island has ever talked about it. They are an entire population of short-sleeved, croquet-playing, backyard gardeners who have never seen a coat or mittens. One day, a man from northern Finland makes an emergency landing of his single-engine plane on the island. After getting out of his aircraft, the man looks at the shocked faces staring back at him and says, "My, it certainly is warm here!" (He says this in Finnish, but that doesn't matter, because they won't know what he means anyway, even if he were speaking their language.) The point is, it feels warm to him, because he knows what cold feels like.

The idea of Good without Evil reminds me of the fish that has never been out of the ocean, or the island where the temperature never changes. Without contrast, without something that's different, there's no way to identify a condition.

Now let's imagine some time in the future when Evil has been eliminated, but people still have some understanding of the concept. Books and movies exist showing what we were like in the early years of the twenty-first century. The front pages of daily newspapers from our time are laminated and mounted on classroom walls, so schoolchildren can learn about the horrors of the past. Families on vacation visit museums that are devoted entirely to Evil. There are even Evil deniers, conspiracy theorists who claim it's all a hoax and that such a thing could never have existed.

Is that really how it would be? More likely, if we could get rid of Evil, the Good that remained would be divided into different grades of good. Eventually, the bottom of the scale would be considered Evil ("What? You only did fifty-two hours of volunteer work last week? What kind of monster are you?"), and we'd be right back where we started. Except without the wars and the murders and the child abuse.

No, I don't think Good can exist without Evil. They are two sides of the same thing, each necessary for the other's existence. But here's an experiment we could try:

We start with a group of some social mammal, maybe prairie dogs. They seem to have developed a complex system of cooperation in which they keep each other out of danger by warning the group when a predator is approaching. If we think of the predator as Evil and the prairie dog group as Good, what would happen if we removed the predators completely? Isolate the prairie dogs inside some kind of protective bubble, where they have food, water, and air -- but no threat. Would they live happily ever after? Or would they eventually turn on each other? Would we see Evil return, springing from within Good itself?

General Rules for the Essay

Here are a few suggestions -- guidelines rather than rules -- based partly on the revised essay on page 101. Keep them in mind as you write.

• Begin with a clearly-expressed rewording of the assigned question. You may also present a thesis statement, a distillation of your position on the issue, which you then explain and support in the rest of the piece.

• Vary the length of your paragraphs, and provide smooth and logical transitions between each paragraph and the next one. I inserted the sentence *Is that really how it would be?* at the beginning of the seventh paragraph because it created a nice bridge between the previous paragraph and the next sentence.

• Do the same with sentences: vary the lengths and create transitions. A lot of short sentences in a row will make your writing sound choppy. A lot of long sentences will exhaust the reader, and your main points will get lost along the way. In the paragraph about the island, I broke one of the sentences into two shorter ones, just to vary the rhythm. In the second-to-the-last paragraph, I originally had three short sentences in a row. I didn't like the way they read, so I combined two of them.

• When possible, use fewer words to say the same thing. Tight writing is usually better. In the second paragraph, I replaced *hold onto* with *retain*. On the other hand, sometimes a few more details strengthens your work. If you have more information and it adds something, put it in. But be careful: don't pad just to fill space! We've all read books that should have been magazine articles.

• Avoid repeating the same word or phrase too many times. In the boxed paragraph at the top of page 99, I used the phrase *single-engine plane*. In the very next sentence, I noticed that I had used the word *plane* again, and replaced it with *aircraft*. In the first two paragraphs of the essay, the word *question* kept trying to work its way into the writing. I deleted it several times.

• Write a little long, then make selective deletions to tighten up your work. That's much better than writing too little and having to puff it up.

• Be just organized enough that you know where you're headed, but flexible enough that you'll discover an unexpected gem or two along the way. Use that big middle section -- the body of your essay -- to develop your ideas.

• Try to end your essay by tying back into what you said in that first paragraph. That will create the impression of organization and completion.

• The finished essay on page 101 is a little longer than I thought it would be. If you're taking the SAT, you won't have time to write and revise an essay of that length. On a timed standardized test, they're looking for a good first draft: Is the writing well-organized, are your points clearly-stated, were you careful about spelling, grammar, and usage, and did you complete the assignment? One more time: Don't give a great answer to the wrong question!

Ready for another?

Let's try a second essay. Before we begin, though, let's address an important question: Is it ever a good idea to try something creative and unexpected when composing an essay, or is it always better to take the safe path?

As with many rules of writing, it depends. On a standardized test, the people judging your essay aren't looking for sparkling wit or a shocking opinion. They aren't even looking for great writing. Once again, you can get a top score by producing a good essay, one that is well-organized, exhibits a competent command of the language, and follows the assignment. Anything more is icing. I'm not saying you shouldn't be creative; I'm saying you shouldn't be creative at the risk of sacrificing those other things. Don't for one second think to yourself, "Those poor judges, having to read essay after essay that answer the same boring question with the same boring ideas. I know: I'll write something completely off-topic and bizarre! It'll wake them up, they'll have a good laugh, and I'll get my perfect score!

No, you won't. You'll open that envelope, take one look at your writing score, and dissolve into your socks.

An essay for a college application is a different story. There, you're trying to stand out from the crowd. You still want to demonstrate your formal writing skills, but give them something unexpected -- *wonderfully* unexpected, not creepy unexpected. Don't whimsically change point of view and tone to introduce your multiple personalities; they'll all be rejected. The admissions people are looking for intelligent, creative, insightful, ethical, active, social applicants who have the background, personality, accomplishments, communication skills, and motivation to make a positive impact on the school and, in turn, take advantage of the opportunities it offers. (Unless you're really good at basketball, and then you can probably forget all that other stuff.)

Now if you're working on an essay for creative writing class, the boundaries are much wider. The teacher may have given you the freedom to express yourself without limits, and if that's the case, go have fun. Write whatever you feel like writing, in any way you want. But as always, be sure to do the assignment. If you're asked to write a four-page alternate ending to a novel, don't hand in a five-line limerick about your weekend in Tallahassee (no matter how good you think it is).

Remember this: Whatever you're working on, and for whatever reason, almost no one will be as impressed with your writing as you are. Sorry, but it's true. And if you're smart, you'll use that little insight to drive you toward better results. Fix the punctuation. Get rid of that run-on sentence. Delete those extra words. People with good writing skills are an endangered species. Don't go down with the rest of the pack.

Let's go do another fine essay.

Essay 2

> "All men desire to be immortal."
> -- Theodore Parker (1810-1860)

Assignment:
What would you do with the "gift" of immortality, and would eternal life be a gift at all? Compose an essay addressing this question. Be sure to use sound reasoning. You may support your point of view with examples from your studies, observations, and personal experiences.

These essay topics tend to be based on huge issues. They don't ask you to write about your pet salamander, or your favorite breakfast cereal. The question is always about something that requires some thought. In fact, you could spend your whole life thinking about it. The trouble is, if you're taking the SAT, you have only twenty-five minutes. The ACT gives you a half-hour, but still, that's not a lot of time when you're trying to figure out the mysteries of the universe.

The real problem is not coming up with an answer to the question. If someone called you on the phone and asked if you'd like to live forever, you'd say, "Yes, please." But an essay prompt isn't simply yes-or-no. You have to present a coherent, detailed opinion. Your response must be in essay form, with a thesis statement followed by logical development and a satisfying conclusion. It may need to examine opposing arguments, possibly from different points of view. This assignment forces you to think about a very big question and give a very elaborate answer in a very small period of time. That can be intimidating. And annoying.

Let's break it down into a pattern you can use for most essay assignments. I'm not a big fan of outlines, because they turn writing into a methodical process, but in the case of a timed essay, they can be helpful.

It isn't an outline we're after, anyway. It's more of a sequence of events. An outline is like a cake recipe, with all of the ingredients in the correct amounts, and a step-by-step list of instructions. What I'm talking about would sound like this: First, we're going to heat the oven and grease a cake pan. Then we're going to mix the flour, sugar, butter, and eggs in a bowl, pour the batter into the pan, and bake it for thirty-five minutes. When the cake has cooled, we'll add the frosting, sing happy birthday, and stuff our faces. See? That isn't a recipe; it's a general plan. So let's start with a similar plan, only with essay things.

First, we'll rephrase the assigned question so we can answer it on our terms (taking care not to change its original meaning or intent).

> If I had the gift of immortality, what would I do with it? Would I think of it as a gift?

Then, we'll interpret the question. This gives us a choice of several different possible paths to follow.

> What do we mean by *immortality*? The physical body living forever? Some kind of life after death, like an immaterial soul? Or is it that we'd be *remembered* forever?

We don't have any way of knowing what Theodore Parker meant by immortality, but because of the time constraint, we'll have to figure out what *we* mean by it. After listing the different paths, we'll choose one, giving ourselves a narrower topic to address. (If we try to say everything, we'll end up with a jumbled mess, and it'll seem as though we've said nothing.)

> Parker lived in the mid-1800s, so I'd guess he was talking about the immortality of the soul. Because he didn't make it past his own 50th birthday, it's obvious he didn't achieve physical immortality. And even though he's famous enough to be quoted, I have no idea who he was, so he's not going to be remembered forever, either. (At least not by me). In any case, I think it would be interesting to talk about living forever in the physical sense.

We also have to be careful not to be *too* narrow. For example, we could talk just about the wonderful things associated with living forever, but the essay would seem incomplete. With any thought at all, we can see that there would be some unpleasant conditions; it might even be unbearable.

> Advantages of living forever (physically):
> - never have to deal with death
> - always more time to do things
> - get to see what will happen in the distant future
> - fame and fortune
>
> Disadvantages:
> - loved ones would all die
> - need to keep starting new families and making new friends
> - run out of things to do
> - constantly adjusting to changing world
> - forever is *forever* -- boring?

Conclusion:
Immortality in the physical sense would be great in the beginning, but the novelty would wear off. Then what?

> All things considered, living forever wouldn't be much fun. It might seem like a gift at first, but eventually it would become a curse, and an eternal one at that.

Again let's start by restating the original question, and establishing the voice and tone of the essay. I'm shooting for serious and light at the same time. That's tricky but I think it can work, because the assignment is both profound and ridiculous.

I don't think I like the title -- mildly clever, but doesn't say anything

> **Immortality: No End in Sight**
> Immortality? Of course! Who wouldn't want to live forever? But how would I use my never-ending time? Would it really be such a ~~welcome~~ gift?

Now I want to set the boundaries for the subject of this essay. What are we going to discuss, and what are we not going to discuss? In this particular case, how will we define immortality?

So many

Michelangelo

> ~~That's a lot of~~ questions. And there are more. For example, what do we mean by immortality? Are we talking about the physical body living forever? Is it immortality in the religious sense, the eternal life of the soul after the body dies? Or ~~is it eternal life~~ in the historical sense, existing forever in the memories of the living (like George Washington or Cleopatra)?

I think it would be a good idea to refer to Theodore Parker, the source of the quote. I'll try to figure out what he meant by immortality. In the process, I'll choose which aspect of eternal life I want to talk about.

forever, barely making it to age fifty.

Too many questions! Change to: I don't see the appeal.

> It's apparent that Theodore Parker didn't live forever; he barely made it to fifty. And he hasn't exactly lived on in our memories either. (Who was he?) I would assume Parker was referring to the immortal soul, but that doesn't seem like an interesting prospect. For one thing, if I have an immortal soul, so does everyone else. I'd just be one more little soul, flitting around in a swarm of billions. What's the appeal?

Once I've identified which path I want to follow, we can be on our way. I have to make sure I give good reasons for my choice, so we can forget about the other options and move ahead. If you read the next paragraph, you'll see that I'm choosing the path and I'm starting to write the main part of the essay at the same time.

attractive.

> Now physical immortality, avoiding death, sounds pretty (great.) There would be no need to ever worry about getting some terminal disease, no more wondering if that persistent cough might be something serious. I'd have an endless amount of time to do things. Isn't that the problem ~~we have~~ with death? We think about all the things we never got to do? And I'd be alive to see what the world is like in two hundred, five hundred, ten thousand years. That would be amazing! I'd go everywhere and see absolutely everything.

travel

The previous paragraph contained all positive aspects of immortality. In the next paragraph, I want to phase into the negative. I won't do it right at the beginning, because that would be too abrupt. But somewhere near the middle, I'll mention one or two unpleasant things.

> Of course, I would be one of a select few enjoying this gift of immortality. Maybe the only (one, and I'd) be famous. I'd probably even get my own television show, and it would become the longest-running show in history. If everyone (was) immortal, I'd just be part of the swarm again. Besides, the world would quickly fill up with people. We'd run out of food and water. Worse, we'd have to carpool. No, everyone else would ~~have to~~ live their lives, then die. As I went on, year after year and decade after decade, I'd have to watch ~~helplessly~~ as my family and friends all passed away. I guess I'd eventually make new friends and start new families, but again, they would die someday, too.

— *one. I'd...*
— *were*

The idea is that these disadvantages will lead into the next paragraph, which will be completely negative.

> Meanwhile, I might start running out of things to do. ~~I mean,~~ how many hobbies can you have? As the centuries passed, I might even see my country disappear, taken over by some hostile nation. And at some point, maybe thousands of years from now, Earth would be hit by that big rock the tabloids keep talking about, and all life would be wiped out. Except for me. I've always been pretty much of a loner, but that still sounds really bad.

And this leads nicely into the conclusion.

> Even if all of those terrible things never happened, what would eternal life be like? Would it be endlessly-exciting? Or just endless? I think immortality (would) seem to be a wonderful gift at first. But soon I would recognize it as a gift I can never return.

— *might*

Writing Rules! 107

Eternal Life: Gift or Curse?

Immortality? Of course! Who wouldn't want to live forever? But how would I use my never-ending time? Would it really be such a gift?

So many questions. And there are more. For example, what do we mean by immortality? Are we talking about the physical body living forever? Is it immortality in the religious sense, the eternal life of the soul after the body dies? Or in the historical sense, existing forever in the memories of the living (like Michelangelo or Cleopatra)?

It's apparent that Theodore Parker didn't live forever, barely making it to age fifty. And he hasn't exactly lived on in our memories either. (Who was he?) I would assume Parker was referring to the immortal soul, but that doesn't seem like an interesting prospect. For one thing, if I have an immortal soul, so does everyone else. I'd just be one more little soul, flitting around in a swarm of billions. I don't see the appeal.

Now physical immortality, avoiding death, sounds pretty attractive. There would be no need to ever worry about getting some terminal disease, no more wondering if that persistent cough might be something serious. I'd have an endless amount of time to do things. Isn't that the problem with death? We think about all the things we never got to do? And I'd be alive to see what the world is like in two hundred, five hundred, ten thousand years. That would be amazing! I'd travel everywhere and see absolutely everything.

Of course, I would be one of a select few enjoying this gift of immortality. Maybe the only one. (I'd be famous. I'd probably even get my own television show, and it would become the longest-running show in history.) If everyone were immortal, I'd just be part of the swarm again. Besides, the world would quickly fill up with people. We'd run out of food and water. Worse, we'd have to carpool. No, everyone else would live their lives, then die. As I went on, year after year and decade after decade, I'd have to watch as my family and friends all passed away. I guess I'd eventually make new friends and start new families, but again, they would die someday, too.

Meanwhile, I might start running out of things to do. How many hobbies can you have? As the centuries passed, I might even see my country disappear, taken over by some hostile nation. And at some point, maybe thousands of years from now, Earth would be hit by that big rock the tabloids keep talking about, and all life would be wiped out. Except for me. I've always been pretty much of a loner, but that still sounds really bad.

Even if all of those terrible things never happened, what would eternal life be like? Would it be endlessly-exciting? Or just endless? I think immortality might seem to be a wonderful gift at first. But soon I would recognize it as a gift I can never return.

Before & After

Here is the first draft of an essay, followed by a rewrite. The assignment was to discuss our planet's limited resources, and whether or not we owe it to future generations to conserve. I haven't marked up the first draft or provided any commentary. Can you figure out why I made the changes?

We hear alot about the planet's dwindling natural resources. We're cutting down all the trees, using up all the oil, and much of our clean water gets wasted. One question is, do we have an obligation to our children and their children to slow down our use of these resources, and I believe we have a definite obligation.

Looking down at the Earth from outer space, the planet looks big, its resources are finite. Simple math tells us that if they use oil at a certain constant rate, and we divide that rate into the amount of oil there is, you have a number of days left before you run out. If we use eighty million barrels every day, and there are a trillion barrels left that we will be able to find and extract, we will only be out of oil in thirty-five years.

Of course, the issue is more complex then that. As we gradually discover and phase in alternative ways of energy, our use of oil will have declined in some places. But as the population of less-affluent nations grow, they're use of petroleum may increase. At the same time, as supplies shrink, prices will go up, which may permit more expensive methods of extraction to be used. The truth is, since no one knows how much oil is left in the ground or how quickly we will use it up. But by treating fuel as a limited resource and adopt reasonable conservation practices, we will achieve success in giving future generations more time to make the necessary discoveries and changes needed to move away from our economy which is so based on oil. After all, its our future to!!!!

We hear a lot about the planet's dwindling resources. We're cutting down the trees, using up the oil, and running out of clean water. Do we have an obligation to future generations to slow down our use of these resources? I believe we do.

If we look down at the Earth from a nearby point in space we are reminded that, although the planet is big, its resources are finite. For example, simple math tells us that if we use oil at a certain constant rate, and we divide that rate into the amount of oil there is, we have a number of days left before we run out. If we use eighty million barrels every day, and there are a trillion barrels left that we can find and extract, we will be out of oil in only thirty-five years.

Of course, the issue is more complex than that. As we discover and phase in alternative sources of energy, our use of oil will decline in some places. But as the populations of less-affluent nations grow, *their* use of petroleum may increase. At the same time, as supplies shrink, prices will go up, which may permit more expensive methods of extraction.

The truth is, no one knows how much oil is left or how quickly we'll use it up. But it's clear that we should treat fuel as a limited resource and adopt reasonable conservation practices. By doing so, we will succeed in giving future generations more time to make the changes needed to move away from our oil-based economy.

Rules We Don't Need

Some high school English teacher somewhere in my life taught the class that we were never to begin a sentence or a paragraph with the words *and* or *but*. Never! Teachers are still peddling this rule, because that's what they were told by their teachers. Here's what I think about it.

Let's consider the word *but*, a conjunction. It connects two ideas in a sentence: the one that was just said and the one coming up. For example:

"We were going to invite you over for dinner, but then we remembered what happened the last time."

If you were going to start a sentence with the word *but*, its function would be to connect its own sentence with the previous one. Again, example:

"Jim, I was driving down our street when I saw a large metallic object, maybe eighty feet across, hovering over your house and sucking up furniture and appliances and also your two dogs in this intense beam of orange light. But that isn't what I came here to tell you."

Do you see how those two sentences need that big pause in between? I suppose you could combine the two, separated by a comma, but the effect would be lost. The first sentence has too much information as it is.

What about starting a paragraph with *but*? Same idea. The first sentence of the new paragraph would have to refer back to the entire previous paragraph. Here, look:

"Hank spent several hours a day visualizing his future career as a major league baseball player. After working his way up through the minors, he'd be signed by some ballclub in the midwest, where he would be a star player on a losing team. He'd lead the league in batting average and home runs for three or four straight years. Then, when his contract was up, Hank would declare himself a free agent and be offered a huge contract to join the New York Yankees. There, he'd be an instant favorite of the fans, enjoy his best years as a player, break tons of records, and eventually be elected to the Hall of Fame.

"But there was one problem. Hank was sixty-two years old."

Again, that last sentence could be tacked onto the end of the previous paragraph, but setting it off by itself helps create the surprise. Also, we have a long, dream-filled first paragraph followed by that short dose of reality. Setting it up this way presents the contrast in a visual way. As the reader, you can *see* how pathetic Hank is as he labors under the sheer weight of his fantasy life.

I'm not saying you should go out of your way to begin a sentence or paragraph with a conjunction. I'm just saying you can, if you do it correctly and for a good reason. (If it makes your writing stronger, that's a good reason.)

Here's another rule I heard over and over from teachers, and maybe you have, too: *Never end a sentence with a preposition.* Really? Why not? Those same teachers did it all the time:

> "Ralph, where did that paper airplane come from?"
> "I'm sorry, Randall, but I have no idea what you're talking about."
> "Excuse me, Mary Louise, what are you laughing at?"
> "I know it's ninety-nine degrees in here, but we don't have air conditioning, so it's something we'll just have to live with."

Those sentences, spoken or written correctly, would sound awkward:

> "Ralph, from where did that paper airplane come?"
> "Excuse me, Mary Louise, at what are you laughing?"
> "I'm sorry, Randall, but I have no idea about what you're talking."
> "I know it's ninety-nine degrees in here, but we don't have air conditioning, so it's something with which we'll just have to live."

Here's another. *Never begin a sentence with a pronoun.* Most of these silly rules have their origin in something legitimate. For example, if placing the pronoun at the beginning of a sentence causes confusion, that's not good:

> "I'm sorry, Mrs. Flannery. Your husband brought your cocker spaniel in for his shots this morning, and on their way out the front door they tripped and fell off the porch. He's near death, I'm afraid."

The problem is, trying to avoid beginning a sentence with a pronoun can force you into using the same noun repeatedly. Your readers won't like that.

There are many other rules that don't deserve to be repeated, but are taught every day in classrooms all over the English-speaking world. Some are debatable. Some aren't. One of my favorites is the rule that says you can't write a paragraph with just one sentence.

Now that's just dumb.

Writing Rules!

A Few More Suggestions and Reminders

☐ Vary the length of sentences and paragraphs. You know from your own reading that a solid mass of words on a page is intimidating. Having more paragraphs tends to create more white space, which invites the eye to come in and look around. Too many long sentences, cluttered with looping clauses, can tire out your reader and garble your message. Good writing contains everything that needs to be said, and nothing else.

☐ Use active verbs whenever possible. Listen to the difference:

"Our hair was scorched by the flames when the explosion of the oil stove took place." (*passive*)

"The oil stove exploded, and the flames scorched our hair." (*active*)

☐ Be consistent with verb tenses. Here's what not to do:

"I walked into the bank to exchange a roll of nickels. Just then, two men wearing ski masks run past me. I tackled them and hold them down. The police had arrived about ten minutes later and say I'm brave, but that I shouldn't be risking my life. The next day I was in the newspaper and everyone thinks I'm a hero."

☐ Be consistent with point of view. Don't mix *one* with *you*, and don't change from first-person to third-person halfway through your story.

☐ English has an incredible variety of words, so there's no need to use the same ones over and over. See if you find this as annoying as I do:

"The landlord refused to return my security deposit, even though when I left, the apartment was in better condition than it had been when I moved in. I asked several times for my deposit back, but he kept refusing. When I asked him why he was refusing to return my deposit, he refused to tell me."

☐ Don't pad your writing just to fill space. It's usually preferable to say something with fewer words. For example, *perfectly round three-dimensional object* is okay; *globe* is better. On the other hand, some detail is good. I'd rather read about "a tiny squirrel, its gray fur flattened, seeking shelter from the biting wind" than "an animal hiding from the storm."

☐ Don't use foreign phrases if you can help it -- especially Latin and French. They're pretentious and distracting. You also risk alienating your reader, who may not know Latin or French. *Capisce?*

☐ Don't add *-wise* to the ends of words. ("I'll try to help you build your gazebo, but I'm really not very experienced, carpentry-wise.") It's lazy and suggests a limited vocabulary. Get yourself a dictionary and a thesaurus.

☐ Don't use idiotic words, such as *ginormous* and *bazillion*.

☐ Some words look like they mean something other than what they actually mean. If you're not absolutely sure about a word, don't use it. Here are a few examples:

restive -- impatient, jittery, or tense
noisome -- offensive; nauseating
quiescent -- still; inactive
bemused -- baffled, confused, or lost in thought
dissemble -- to pretend; to behave dishonestly
enervate -- to weaken physically, mentally, or morally
disinterested -- impartial

One More Time

☐ The past tense of the verb *lead* is *led*.

☐ You infer a meaning from something you read or hear. It's the reader or listener who *infers*; the writer or speaker *implies*.

☐ Don't use *there's* when you mean *there are*:

"It's possible that there's a chipmunk living in my car."
"I think there are three bowling alleys on this block alone."

☐ Make sure you can use these correctly. Please!

Your and *you're*
There, *their*, and *they're*
Its and *it's*

Writing Rules!

A or B

Each of the numbered boxes below contains a pair of sentences. One of the sentences in each pair is correct as written, while the other has at least one error. Put a check in the box corresponding to the **correct** sentence. Answers are on page 117.

1.
   - [A] The wind blew off Sid's hairpiece and one of the other hunters shot it.
   - [B] Gladys looked at her new driver's license photo, she demanded a refund.

2.
   - [A] I couldn't decide between lemon cake or chocolate ice cream, so I had both.
   - [B] Pete and Sam were asleep at their desks when the boss walked in.

3.
   - [A] We appreciate you listening and hope you'll tune in again tomorrow.
   - [B] Following an elliptical path, Earth takes 365 days to orbit the sun.

4.
   - [A] Ann's collection of rare pillowcases were stolen during the riot.
   - [B] The DVD player fell down three flights of stairs, but seems to be all right.

5.
   - [A] It was the fourth inning; he went for a hot dog and never came back.
   - [B] Please except our sincere apologies for the hole in your roof.

6.
   - [A] That U-turn on the bridge was the reason why you failed your road test.
   - [B] I don't remember eating the whole pizza, but I guess I did.

7.
   - [A] The population of New York is bigger than any other city in the country.
   - [B] If you want to lose your money, a casino is a good place to do it.

8.
   - [A] I'm flattered, Mark, but please don't name your pet walrus after me.
   - [B] Evonne's favorite subjects are math, science, and studying literature.

9.
   - [A] He started a fire with his shirt, it being the only combustible item around.
   - [B] They're not going to appreciate where you mounted their satellite dish.

10.
    - [A] In an election between Albert and me, I would wipe the floor with him.
    - [B] If a mountain lion approaches, just remain stationery and try not to cry.

Writing Rules!

Which Word?

All possible answers are at left. Correct answers are on page 117.

antidote anecdote tenet tenant martial marshal discreet discrete uninterested disinterested elude allude infer imply lead led effect affect adverse averse pore pour incite insight cemetery parallel baited separate compliment complement lend loan lose loose principal principle hearty hardy waive wave eager anxious liable libel advice advise pique peak

Across
1. Make complete
3. A deep understanding
4. Used to keep track of dates
7. Read or study carefully
8. Bored
11. To give, but expecting payback
12. Describes lines that never meet
16. Principle or belief
17. A resting place, finally
20. Misplace
22. Unwilling, resistant
23. Related to fighting
24. To voluntarily relinquish
26. Reduced in intensity
27. Restrained or tactful

Down
2. A rule, law, or guideline
5. Short story based on a real event
6. Arouse or annoy
9. Make an indirect statement
10. Of *alright* and *already*, the one that's a real word
13. A helpful suggestion
14. The publication of malicious lies about someone
15. Past tense of *lead*
18. To escape
19. Durable
21. Pull apart
22. Of *anxious* and *eager*, the one that means uneasy
25. To have an impact

Writing Rules!

Too late, and poorly written.

George and I felt badly that we didn't make it to your Groundhog Day party. We received the invitation in the mail, but put it on the kitchen counter as a reminder. Then I guess we got used to it being there, and after a while it just blended into the background. When the cat knocked the invitation onto the floor this morning, I picked it up and seen the date. I could of died of embarrassment. I felt like we had let you down. Please don't use this as a reason to not invite George and I to your April Fool's Day formal dinner dance. We'll even make that incredulous coconut cucumber cake you love. Is it still your favorite desert? Believe it or not, I can't wait until we're altogether again.

The note at left contains several errors. In fact, each of the ten sentences has one. Write your corrections in the spaces below, then check your answers on page 117.

1. _____
2. _____
3. _____
4. _____
5. _____
6. _____
7. _____
8. _____
9. _____
10. _____

We need order.

The following paragraph doesn't contain any grammatical errors (I hope), but the sentences are not in the best order. Rearrange the sentences by number so the paragraph makes sense.

(1) We know that the greater the mass of a body, the greater the gravitational force it exerts. (2) Nobody knows! (3) Gravity is one of the great mysteries of science. (4) But how exactly does one physical body tug at another across millions of miles of space? (5) Jupiter's gravity is stronger than Pluto's.

Who wants an apostrophe?

Four of the following underlined words are correct as written. Which four?

That truck seems to be missing <u>it's</u> left front tire. I believe this toothbrush is <u>yours</u>. Our house looks like a tool shed compared to <u>their's</u>. My <u>aunt's</u> hair is pink. I don't like those <u>cow's</u> walking across our lawn. Where is the <u>men's</u> department? <u>There's</u> a mosquito on your ear. Who <u>know's</u> where Ecuador is?

Writing Rules!

Answers
Pages 114-116

A or B
1. A 2. B 3. B 4. B 5. A 6. B 7. B 8. A 9. B 10. A

Which Word?

Across
1. COMPLEMENT
3. INSIGHT
4. CALENDAR
7. PORE
8. UNINTERESTED
11. LEND
12. PARALLEL
16. TENET
17. CEMETERY
20. LOSE
22. AVERSE
23. MARTIAL
24. WAIVE
26. BATED
27. DISCREET

Down
2. PRINCIPLE
5. ANECDOTE
6. PIQUE
9. IMPLY
10. ALREADY
13. ADVICE
14. LIBEL
15. LED
18. ELUDE
19. HARDY
21. SEPARATE
22. ANXIOUS
25. AFFECT

Too late, and poorly written.
1. bad (not *badly*)
2. and (not *but*)
3. its being there (not *it being there*)
4. saw (not *seen*)
5. could have (not *could of*)
6. as if or as though (not *like*)
7. George and me (not *George and I*)
8. incredible (not *incredulous*)
9. dessert (not *desert*)
10. all together (not *altogether*)

We need order.
3, 1, 5, 4, 2

Who wants an apostrophe?
yours, aunt's, men's, There's

What is writing made of?

Or, if we must follow that silly rule about not ending a sentence with a preposition, Of what is writing made? What are the building blocks, the essential elements, of good writing?

I would say there are at least five.

First, there has to be something you want to say. You need a message, a story, an opinion, a theory, an observation -- some reason for writing.

Second, you need structural boundaries. When an architect is hired to design a building, the people financing the project don't say, "Create whatever you want, on any scale, with any budget, and at any location." There are requirements and limitations; in other words, there are rules. I've tried to present at least a good sampling of the rules for writing in this book. (There are quite a few more.)

Third, you want access to the vast variety of words in the English language. The stronger your vocabulary, the more interesting and precise your writing will be. You'll be able to create images in your readers' minds, identify subtle traits and meaning, and say exactly what you mean. Or at least closer to what you mean than you could with a smaller vocabulary.

I'm not talking about showing off, or using big words just for the sake of using big words. That won't impress anyone, and will probably irritate a few

people. As I said earlier regarding Latin and other foreign phrases: avoid them whenever possible. In the same way, avoid obscure words that will send your reader scrambling for the dictionary, or for something else to read. If the person on the other end doesn't know what you're saying, the mind-to-mind connection won't happen. And in that case, you're wasting your time. Not to mention expensive toner.

Fourth, you need a voice. What do you sound like to your reader? I have no way of being sure about this, but I think a writer's voice develops over time. If you try to assume a voice, the way you put on a coat, it will feel uncomfortable to you, and artificial to the person reading your words. This will almost certainly be true if you try to adopt another writer's voice. The more you write, the more you will grow into your natural voice, and the less you will even think about it as you work.

The fifth thing you need is knowledge. Read and learn as much as you can about the world, other people, cultures, nature, philosophy, and whatever interests you. It isn't that you'll necessarily be writing about those subjects (although you may). It's that writing is like hang gliding. Rising warm air, called a thermal, is what keeps a hang glider soaring. Knowledge is a writer's thermal. The oldest adage for aspiring writers is: "Write what you know." If that's good advice, then the more you know, the more you'll write. What may be surprising, but just as true, is that the more you write, the more you'll learn. I've certainly learned a lot while writing this book.

It's a cycle, really. As we grow as individuals, we come to understand ourselves a little better, so we're better able to communicate our ideas. Those ideas become part of the external world, where they are mixed with the ideas of other people. We take in new information, shake it around, recombine it in creative ways, and the cycle continues.

The secret to good writing, then, is to keep your eyes and ears open and your feet moving. Don't fall too deeply in love with your own thoughts, stay open to always learning something new, be ready to share what you know and to hear what others know, and try never to coast too long.

One more thing. Remember that when you read the work of a published writer, you're seeing the finished product. You never see the first, second, third, and fourth drafts that ended up in the garbage. You have no idea if an editor made suggestions and changes, or how many friends and family members read earlier versions and offered feedback. You don't know if a proofreader caught and corrected dozens of mistakes. You're seeing only the polished jewel. I said this earlier, but it's worth repeating. Don't judge any writing project by your first attempt. Most writers would do anything to avoid letting you see the early stages of something they've written. I know I would.

I'd even have a fluoride treatment.

I hope you enjoyed this book. Don't forget to write!

Four more books by the same author:

500 Key Words for the SAT* and How To Remember Them Forever!

Uses visual images and funny stories to build a bridge between each unfamiliar word and its meaning. Also points out look-alike and sound-alike words, and provides alternate parts of speech and sample sentences. More than 100 cartoons and a section on strategies for the SAT add to the effectiveness of this powerful vocabulary-building tool.

(Softcover, 120 pages, $12.95)

100 Math Tips for the SAT* and How To Master Them Now!

Does more than teach you how to solve the problem. It teaches you how to *see* the problem, how to recognize traps, and how to think. Filled with straight talk, solid information, humor, clear diagrams, cartoons, additional practice questions, and a complete glossary. There's math, and there's SAT math. A good score comes from knowing the difference!

(Softcover, 120 pages, $12.95)

Please visit our website for information on purchasing these books.

One Thousand Words

No jokes, no cartoons, no fooling around. Just a thousand (actually eleven hundred) words, their meanings, pronunciation, parts of speech, and clear sentences that will help you really understand. A companion to *500 Key Words for the SAT*, with little overlap, and an excellent source for any standardized test.

(Softcover, 120 pages, $9.95)

Learn This! (Stuff You Need to Know, and Mistakes You Need to Stop Making, Before You Step Foot into High School)

Geography, history, math, science, writing, music & art, literature, world religions & languages, and more. Also provides a systematic method for learning. Packed with great stuff!

(Softcover, 64 pages, $8.95)

Call toll-free, or visit us online:

Mostly Bright Ideas
888-301-2829
888-832-6483 (fax)
http://www.mostlybrightideas.com

---

*SAT is a registered trademark of the College Entrance Examination Board, which does not endorse these products.

www.ingramcontent.com/pod-product-compliance
Lightning Source LLC
Chambersburg PA
CBHW081458040426
42446CB00016B/3296